MANY ROOMS

INSIDE A WOMAN'S HEART

Debbie Snyder

Many Rooms Inside a Woman's Heart
Copyright © 2006 by Debbie Snyder

ISBN: 1-59352-268-1

Published by Christian Services Network
833 Broadway, Suite 201
El Cajon, CA 92021
Toll Free: 1-866-484-6184
www.CSNbooks.com

Printed in the United States of America

DEDICATION

The reason I named this book *Many Rooms Inside a Woman's Heart* is that I truly believe God has given women such a tremendous capacity to love and serve in so many areas of people's lives. Inside the heart is the core of all women, the very substance that makes us what and who we are.

I would first like to dedicate this book to my mother, Sally, who is my best friend and loved me unconditionally all of my life. Also, to my husband Rex, my son Eric and my two daughters, Paige and Sarah, to my son-in-law Ryan and my grandsons Denver and Samuel – all of whom I cannot imagine my life without. To my brothers, Ray & Van, whose prayers and lives encourage me daily in my Christian walk. To my pastor, Steve, of over 20 years, who has loved and prayed for our family – you have been such a strong support for me and taught me many valuable truths. And to my friend, Irene, who took time to read my first writings and encourage me to go forward – I thank you for believing in me.

There are so many people who have touched my life in different ways that are not mentioned in this book. Thank you to ALL the rest of my family whom I dearly love and pray for every day; to every woman who has shown me love and compassion, taught me to reach out beyond myself, stretched me further than I thought possible and prayed for me to know the most incredible, unconditional love: that of the heavenly Father, I thank You.

The most important goal I have for everything I have written is to touch the lives of those who read it and draw them to a closer walk with an all knowing, all powerful, all healing and almighty God. To Him be ALL the glory, the honor and praise, for He alone is worthy.

TABLE OF CONTENTS

CHAPTER ONE

The Joy of Womanhood

God's Word tells us that women were purposefully
created. What we do with what we are given defines
who we become. Lord, make me a woman
of great purpose!
Use the circumstances of my life to mold me
into who I was created to be.

Inside a Woman's Heart

Let's start out with a really big word: WOMAN.

WOW!

I feel so blessed and proud to be one.

Celebrate!

The Bible says God created a deep sleep to come upon Adam, and while he slept, God took one of his ribs and closed up the flesh in its place. From this rib He made woman to be bone of his bones, flesh of his flesh. She was called "woman" because she was taken out of man.

Women, we have reason to celebrate! Man was not complete without God adding OUR unique design to complete him. Just think about it: we were designed for a purpose, created for a plan, glorious to behold.

We are everything and nothing apart from the Master's hand. As He breathed the breath of life into our being, so does He also desire to breathe the breath of life into our very souls and spirits to make us beautiful creations in His sight.

Embrace the Journey

I hope that as you read this book, you can identify with the stories and feelings of the woman you are, the woman you once were and the woman you may want to become.

Womanhood is a journey, a way of life, that embraces continually looking inside our hearts and seeking to be the woman God wants us to be. May the prayer of each of our lips be:

Open the eyes of my heart Lord,
open the eyes of my heart.
I want to see You.
I want to know You.

(Words by Paul Baloche)

INFLUENCE FOR GOOD

One thing I realize more and more the older I get is that we are responsible for the influence we pass on to all the people in our lives with whom we touch shoulders. It is a humbling thing to think about. Not only will we answer for our own actions, but for the way in which we helped to shape or influence other lives as well.

Looking back, I wish I had had more time to spend with some of the women in my life, to listen to their hearts and learn the wisdom they could impart to me. Two such women were my grandmothers. They both died while I was still in elementary school, and although they were very different women, they both had hearts for God and lived Christian lives. I feel so connected to them both because we all shared the forgiving grace and mercy of our heavenly Father.

A WONDERFUL HERITAGE

Unfortunately, one of my grandfathers drank a lot. I remember as a young girl, I would walk down the lane from our house to theirs to find Grandma with her long hair tied up in a bun and long dress on, canning and boiling jar after jar of produce from the garden and putting it on shelves in the cellar pantry. Then my grandfather would come home and in a fit of rage pull the tablecloth out from under everything, and all of her hard work and efforts would be gone in a moment's time.

I think what I remember most of Grandma Jacobs was a humble and quiet spirit, a love that was rooted and grounded in truth so deep I knew it came from God.

What a wonderful heritage for me!

In the last years of my grandfather's life, he gave his heart to Christ and I know today it was from all the years of prayer that went up for him from the loving heart of my grandmother, who never gave up.

A GRANDMOTHER'S LOVE

I think of Grandma Westover, who took me to nursing home services to help out with the hymnals, who modeled before me a pleasant and bubbling personality, a sense of humor and a constant smile. She used to comb my long blonde hair one hundred strokes and tell me she thought I was an angel in disguise.

How wonderful that used to make me feel!

I would go with her to different crusade meetings and revivals and I would hear and learn so much about God's love, amazing grace and forgiveness. I never had to question her love for God because her actions spoke loud and clear what was in her heart: the love of God.

THE RICHES OF HIS LOVE

The love of God is so rich and pure; it reaches to the highest mountain and it flows to the lowest valleys. It encompasses the deepest sorrows and rejoices in the greatest victories.

> *But when the fullness of the time had come, God sent forth His son, born of a woman...*
> (Galatians 4:4)

Oh God, let our hearts be like that of Mary when she received the news that she would bear a Son after the Holy Spirit of God came upon her. She replied with a willing heart, *"...Behold the maid servant of the Lord! Let it be to me according to your word..."* (Luke 1:38).

How many times we say to God, "whatever Your will is, Lord"... but do we really mean it?

> *Have Thine own way Lord,*
> *have Thine own way.*
> *Thou are the potter,*
> *I am the clay.*
> (Words by Adelaide Pollard & George Stebbins)

MANY ROOMS

I believe a woman's heart has many rooms, just as we have many roles to play. We fill them with all kinds of things: jobs, family, marriage, children, God, on and on it goes.

THE HIDDEN PLACES

Sometimes we have rooms that we keep locked up and secretly tucked away from everyone else.

14

Only God can get into the hidden places of your heart. He has access into your very soul. Remember, He is the one who created you and formed you in your mother's womb.

My frame was not hidden from You, when I was made in secret, and skillfully wrought in the lowest parts of the earth. Your eyes saw my substance, being yet unformed...

(Psalm 139:15-16)

Do you have any rooms that do not get much use? In our house we have a formal living room that is pretty to look at, but is not used much except for guests and holiday gatherings. We now have a large, beautiful dining room table in it also, that good friends of mine graciously sent me from their Texas home, and I am currently writing this book on it. Thank you Dick and Marie!

BEHIND CLOSED DOORS

I wonder how many of us have rooms in our hearts with closed doors; places where no one has stepped for a while, the cobwebs are building up and the walls need to be washed down – maybe a fresh coat of paint needs to be applied. God wants to search every corner of our hearts. He wants us to open the door of every room and pull up the shades so His glory can shine in.

What we store up on the inside affects our daily life on the outside. If we are harboring ill feelings of unforgiveness, bitterness and hatred, it is going to be seen by our family and friends. When our spiritual reservoir is empty it affects what people see.

We are told in 1 Peter 3:4 that we are to be beautiful inside our hearts, with the lasting charm of a gentle and quiet spirit that is so precious to God.

A Living Sacrifice

When people look at you, do they see cracked and peeling walls? Or do they see a freshly redecorated room that Christ's love has shone in and cleaned up? Do they see a woman who daily offers her body as a living sacrifice to God?

I know I want to be that kind of woman. I want others to look past my shell and see into my heart. I want them to see Jesus. *"For we are His workmanship, created in Christ Jesus for good works, which God prepared beforehand that we should walk in them"* (Ephesians 2:10).

When Christ redeemed us, He put a new nature within; old things have passed away and all things are new.

Let your light so shine before men, that they may see your good works and glorify your Father in Heaven.
(Matthew 5:16)

Spring Cleaning

Is it time to do a little spiritual spring cleaning?

Search me oh God, and know my heart... and see if there is any wicked way in me.
(Psalm 139:23-24)

Shine Your floodlight right into the very corners of my soul, God, and expose the rooms that I have shut You out

16

of. Make my heart a beautiful castle filled with love, forgiveness and all of the fruits of Your Spirit.

The wise woman builds her house, but the foolish pulls it down with her hands.

(Proverbs 14:1)

DIAMOND IN THE ROUGH

SHINING RADIANTLY

You woke me this morning, Lord, giving me these words: "Diamond in the Rough."

I believe You are speaking about all of the women who are willing to let You take their lives and chip away at them just like a jeweler does a stone, to cut away the imperfections and impurities, and the things that are not pleasing unto You until they are polished and shine radiantly in Your presence.

Just as a diamond is strong and brilliant, so can our lives be in Your sight.

A diamond is a very strong stone. Likewise, I want to be "shatter proof" for Jesus. Psalm 18:2 says, *"The Lord is my rock and my fortress and my deliverer; my God, my strength, in whom I will trust..."*

THE REFINING PROCESS

It is when we allow You to put us through the "refining process": to wash us, purify us and set us apart to be molded into Your image, that we become a brilliant gemstone for Your Kingdom.

You have a mighty arm; strong is Your hand, and high is Your right hand.

(Psalm 89:13)

We are and can be nothing apart from You taking our lives, diamonds in the rough, and molding us, melting us down, shaping us and filling us so that we can be used for Your glory.

Finally my brethren, be strong in the Lord and in the power of His might.

(Ephesians 6:10)

FREE WOMAN

I wonder how many of my readers are wearing shackles. I am not talking about the ones you can see with the naked eye; I am speaking of the ones that are within, that weigh us down and make our hearts feel as if they weigh 100 pounds.

BOUGHT WITH A PRICE

Can you imagine living back in the days of the slaves? I do not think any of us would even like to try. How happy we would be if our master would say that we are free!

It is the same today. Our master is Christ and He is Lord over both the enslaved and the free. He has already paid the price for our freedom, but so many times the key to the shackles is right there before us and we choose not to unlock them. We choose to carry the weights, to bear the sin and shame Christ has already paid for on the cross.

On the cross, Jesus paved the way for us to be freed from the chains of bondage that tie us down and hold us back from being the women He wants us to be, from living spirit-filled lives.

We need to trade our old unregenerate lives in for the new life that leads to everlasting life instead of death.

SURRENDER EQUALS FREEDOM

Satan would love nothing more than to keep you bound and gagged for eternity, but the good news is that Jesus came to set you free! John 8:36 says, *"Therefore if the Son makes you free, you shall be free indeed."*

Who is in control of the hidden places in your heart? God has given you the freedom to choose. Only when you give Him access into your heart can He give liberty to your soul. He turns resentment into grace and anger into forgiveness and love.

My parents used to sing:

> *Shackled 'neath a heavy burden,*
> *beneath a load of guilt and shame.*
> *Then the hand of Jesus touched me*
> *and now I am no longer the same.*
> *He touched me, Oh, He touched me*
> *and oh the joy that floods my soul.*
> *Something happened and now I know.*
> *He touched me and made me whole.*
> (Words by William J. Gaither)

19

TRADE BONDAGE FOR SWEET FREEDOM

Has Jesus touched you? Are you free from the chains of sin and death? Trade your bondage for sweet freedom that will flood your soul with peace!

It does not matter who you are, what you have done, your race, sex, age – none of it matters. We are all one in Christ when we come to the foot of the cross.

You can become free today by the power of His blood.

Sign up!

Freedom is a gift. Just take it, open it and thank God for His amazing grace that paid for it.

> *Yet in all these things we are more than conquerors through Him who loved us. For I am persuaded that neither death nor life, nor angels nor principalities nor powers, nor things present nor things to come, nor height nor depth, nor any other created thing, shall be able to separate us from the love of God which is in Christ Jesus our Lord.*
>
> (Romans 8:37-39)

SEASHELLS

HEARTS OF GOLD

I belong to a ladies' connection group in my church. For one season of each year, we study a book pertaining to women to help us grow spiritually.

In other words, we want to become more like Christ. The name of our group is "Hearts of Gold." Sometimes we laugh, sometimes we cry but always we pray each week as we seek to know God's will for our lives.

Each woman who makes up our circle is unique. I am so thankful to each one for their inspiration to me in my spiritual walk! Just like seashells, we are all different shapes and sizes: some broken, some chipped, some smooth and soft, but ALL women who love the Lord and desire to be picked up and chosen.

USED FOR HIS GLORY

We call these bodies our "shells," use them for Your Kingdom and Your glory, Lord!

Blessed are those who hunger and thirst for righteousness, for they shall be filled.
(Matthew 5:6)

I beseech you therefore, brethren, by the mercies of God, that you present your bodies a living sacrifice, holy, acceptable to God, which is your reasonable service.
(Romans 12:1)

Do you not know that your body is the temple of the Holy Spirit who is in you, whom you have from God, and you are not your own? For you were bought at a price, therefore glorify God in your body and in your spirit, which are God's.
(1 Corinthians 6:19-20)

PAPER DOLL CUTOUTS

I remember loving to play with paper doll cutouts when I was growing up; dressing the hard cardboard figures first this way and then that, accessorizing, changing outfits and basically making my play figures into puppets.

MANY HATS

Now that I am a woman, I realize I wear many "hats" just as those paper dolls did. I am a daughter, mother, wife, friend, neighbor, daughter-in-law, sister, sister-in-law... on and on it goes.

It certainly takes a lot of "costumes" to fill all the roles we play in real life!

Sometimes I feel like a puppet, constantly being pulled by the demands placed on me. I do not think I am alone.

Have you ever felt that way?

INCOGNITO

It would be nice to escape just for a day to an island where no one knows me, to be incognito with a big, wide-brimmed hat and really large sunglasses.

When the world is pressing in on me I am so thankful to remember that I am a child of the Most High, a daughter of the King, a woman cut out, molded and made into the image God created, a beautiful creature in Christ.

I want to be made into His likeness, don't you?

So God created man in His own image; in the image of God He created him; male and female He created them.

(Genesis 1:27)

PILLOW TALK

THE TONE OF PEACE

I was amazed when I realized how many scriptures in the Bible deal with peace. I like to think of the woman of the house setting a tone of peace. I know that it is not always easy: children fight, dinners get burned, things break, bills pile up... on and on it goes. Yet I believe it is our responsibility and privilege as women to be peacemakers.

Even if you are a single woman, I hope you desire a life of peace.

Peace reminds me of a big, fluffy down comforter or a large, puffy water pillow. It envelopes you, surrounds you, comforts you, boosts you up, cushions you, supports you, and leaves you with a feeling the world cannot know. I have had many storms in my life so I am doubly thankful for the peace Christ has placed in my heart.

SHALLOW PROMISES

My husband is a pilot and we have flown many times through the clouds. I always used to think of clouds as these big, soft, puffy wads of cotton that you could probably sit and bounce on. Wrong! According to the dictionary they are merely visible bodies of moisture that can create turbulence when you go through them.

Clouds remind me of the peace the world hands out – shallow commitments and empty promises that do not carry their weight. Only the peace of Christ can take us through the storms that life will bring: shattered dreams, heartaches and loss.

THE GOD OF LOVE AND PEACE

I am so thankful for the peace that "passeth all under-standing!"

And the peace of God, which surpasses all under-standing, will guard your hearts and minds through Christ Jesus.

(Philippians 4:7)

Great peace have those who love Your law, and nothing causes them to stumble.

(Psalm 119:165)

...Become complete. Be of good comfort, be of one mind, live in peace; and the God of love and peace will be with you.

(2 Corinthians 13:11)

Isaiah 9:6 tells us that God's Word, Jesus, is the Prince of Peace. I love that illustration of Christ!

You will keep him in perfect peace, whose mind is stayed on You...

(Isaiah 26:3)

But the fruit of the Spirit is love, joy, peace, long-suffering, kindness, goodness, faithfulness, gentleness and self-control. Against such there is no law.

(Galatians 5:22-23)

Peace I leave with you, My peace I give to you; not as the world gives do I give to you. Let not your heart be troubled, neither let it be afraid.

(John 14:27)

These things I have spoken to you, that in Me you may have peace. In the world you will have tribulation; but be of good cheer, I have overcome the world.

(John 16:33)

If it is possible, as much as depends on you, live peaceably with all men.

(Romans 12:18)

Blessed are the peacemakers, for they shall be called sons of God.

(Matthew 5:9)

Therefore, having been justified by faith, we have peace with God through our Lord Jesus Christ.

(Romans 5:1)

For He Himself is our peace.

(Ephesians 2:14)

And let the peace of God rule in your hearts, to which also you were called in one body; and be thankful.

(Colossians 3:15)

Flee also youthful lusts; but pursue righteousness, faith, love, peace with those who call on the Lord out of a pure heart.

(2 Timothy 2:22)

But the wisdom that is from above is first pure, then peaceable, gentle, willing to yield, full of mercy and good fruits, without partiality and without hypocrisy. Now the fruit of righteousness is sown in peace by those who make peace

(James 3:17-18)

The Real Thing

Do you ever tire of artificial things: fake sweeteners, "almost" butter, substitute salt, and so on? What ever happened to the real thing? And how about real people? I love the song by Casting Crowns that talks about *"all the plastic people under all the shiny plastic steeples."*

Take off the Mask

Do we dare take off our masks and just be who we really are – genuine human beings who have cares, joys, pains, feelings? I think it is refreshing when I meet someone genuine, someone whose body language just says, "Here I am. This is me."

God, help us to be real people. Help us to examine our lives and what we say to the world everyday. Help others to see Your love in us – changed lives, transformed out of darkness into your glorious light.

I want to be the real thing; not a "veneer" Christian, but a blood-bought, sold-out-life for You.

The Sacrifice of Motherhood

God gave much thought to the design and purpose of women as mothers. I believe He knew everything we would need to be "the real thing" to our families. He knew tears would be needed, and forgiveness and compassion. He knew that there would be times of loneliness, pride, joy, sadness, disappointment and pain. Motherhood requires a great deal of sacrifice and willingness to serve.

God knew stress would be part of our lives, so He told us to cast ALL of our cares upon Him because He cares for us and He is wonderfully able to handle everything we give to Him.

Casting all your care upon Him, for He cares for you.
(1 Peter 5:7)

The Lord is good, a stronghold in the day of trouble; and He knows those who trust in Him.
(Nahum 1:7)

I want to be a real woman for Jesus, don't you? Proverbs 31:30 tells us that *"...charm is deceitful and beauty is passing, but a woman who fears the Lord, she shall be praised."*

Let us join together as women of faith to be real to everyone around us.

CHAPTER TWO

Jesus' Gift to Us

Jesus has given us an indescribable gift:
the ability to be reconciled with our Creator.
Father, may I take advantage of ALL You have for me!

THE GIFT

Have you ever received a gift? Something someone gives you just because they want to; because they love and care about you? Isn't it a great feeling?

I love to give gifts. I think I am a more gracious giver than I am a receiver. I just love to pick things up throughout the year and tuck them away so I have them to give when the opportunity arises.

WHAT BETTER GIFT?

I think one of the reasons I love to give is because of everything I have received in my own heart and life through Christ's love for me. What better gift than that of eternal life? John 3:16 says,

> *For God so loved the world that He gave his only begotten Son, that whoever believes in Him should not perish but have everlasting life.*

One of the illustrations our pastor uses for salvation is someone giving you a beautifully wrapped gift which you accept and give thanks for, but then perhaps put on a shelf. If you never unwrap or open it, you can never know the joy of what the giver was offering to you.

That is how it is with salvation. God has given us the gift of eternal life in Christ if we will accept it, thank Him for it and then begin to apply what He has done into our daily lives.

> *For the wages of sin is death, but the gift of God is eternal life in Christ Jesus, our Lord.*
> (Romans 6:23)

GIVING GOOD GIFTS

I believe every woman is a gift-giver of some kind; whether it is through talents, words, or deeds. We all want to please others and be accepted. But none of our gifts can compare to the gift Christ has bought for us.

If you then, being evil, know how to give good gifts to your children, how much more will your Father who is in heaven give good things to those who ask Him.
(Matthew 7:11)

For by grace you have been saved through faith, and that not of yourselves; it is the gift of God.
(Ephesians 2:8)

Every good gift and every perfect gift is from above, and comes down from the Father of lights, with whom there is no variation or shadow of turning.
(James 1:17)

As each one has received a gift, minister it to one another, as good stewards of the manifold grace of God.
(1 Peter 4:10)

SACRIFICE

When you think of the word "sacrifice," what comes to your mind? Giving up a meal, a TV show, passing down things you do not really need or want anymore?

Can you imagine sacrificing one of your children for the sins of the world?

THE LAMB THAT WAS SLAIN

Jesus was the supreme sacrifice, the Lamb that was slain to wash away all of our sins with His blood. He was the perfect lamb without sin, and it is only by His blood that we have forgiveness and reconciliation, access into the very throne of grace.

I am so thankful that the doorpost of my heart is covered with His blood!

Are you thankful for that blood today; the blood that washes us whiter than snow? I love that old song:

> *Oh, the blood of Jesus,*
> *Oh the blood of Jesus,*
> *Oh the blood of Jesus,*
> *It washes white as snow.*

(Artist Unknown)

And the blood of Jesus Christ His son cleanseth us from all sin.

(1 John 1:7)

NOT A PRETTY PICTURE

When we think of "blood," it is not a pretty picture that enters our minds; it is kind of a gory thought. But when I think about Jesus' blood, I think of purity and love, forgiveness and sacrifice. He paid it all — just for me and just for you. Nothing else would do, it is only by His blood are we saved.

Thank God for the blood that covers me!

33

Lord, wash me and make me whiter than snow. I want nothing less.

When you think about the blood of Christ, I hope it will paint a new picture in your mind. Think of it as a flowing fountain of healing and forgiveness through which you and I must travel to become children of God.

Apply It to Your Heart

Are you part of the Body of Christ today? Have you asked Jesus to cover your multitude of sins in the sea of His great love?

If the blood has not been applied to your heart and life today, ask Jesus to come in and cover you with His precious blood.

What are you waiting for?

The sacrifices of God are a broken spirit, a broken and a contrite heart. These, O God, You will not despise.
(Psalm 51:17)

And to love the Lord with all the heart, with all the understanding, with all the soul, and with all the strength, and to love one's neighbor as oneself, is more than all the whole brunt offerings and sacrifices.
(Mark 12:33)

And walk in love, as Christ also has loved us and given Himself for us, an offering and a sacrifice to God for a sweet-smelling aroma.
(Ephesians 5:2)

Jesus came to Earth to accomplish His atoning work: "*...He has appeared to put away sin by the sacrifice of Himself*" (Hebrews 9:26). Then He entered into Heaven, opening the way of access to God.

We need to continually offer up a sacrifice of praise to God. God uses us through the power of the Holy Spirit to produce new and living worship from our mouths and our whole being.

I beseech you therefore, brethren, by the mercies of God, that you present your bodies as a living sacrifice, holy, acceptable to God, which is your reasonable service.

(Romans 12:1)

But if we walk in the light as He is in the light, we have fellowship with one another and the blood of Jesus Christ His Son cleanses us from all sin.

(1 John 1:7)

But now in Christ Jesus you who once were far off have been brought near by the blood of Christ.

(Ephesians 2:13)

...Jesus Christ, the faithful witness, the firstborn from the dead, and the ruler over the kings of the earth. To Him who loved us and washed us from our sins in His own blood.

(Revelation 1:5)

In Him we have redemption through His blood, the forgiveness of sins, according to the riches of His grace.

(Ephesians 1:7)

HEART TRANSPLANT

I have never actually experienced a physical heart transplant surgery, but I have received a spiritual one and I am so thankful for it. I never want to go back to the person I was before the transformation took place! I am so thankful to the hand of the Holy Spirit taking a hold of my heart and changing me into a person He could use.

GENTLE AND LOWLY IN HEART

I want to be like David, who said in Psalm 131:1,

Lord, my heart is not haughty, nor my eyes lofty. Neither do I concern myself with great matters, nor with things too profound for me.

The description Jesus gave of Himself was "gentle and lowly in heart; humble."

> *Oh to be like Jesus,*
> *to be like Jesus,*
> *all I ask*
> *to be like Him.*

Oh that we could learn to quiet our hearts and spirits before our loving God!

HIDE HIS WORD

"For as he thinks in his heart, so is he…" (Proverbs 23:7). This is speaking of the things we digest and feed our minds and souls on. They will surely reflect who we really are.

How careful we should be to hide God's Word in our

36

hearts and to be ready every day to give an answer of the hope that is in us to a lost and hurting world!

"As in water face reflects face, so a man's heart reveals the man" (Proverbs 27:19). I like this verse because it forces me to look inside to see who I really am.

A verse of one of my favorite songs says:

Search me, Oh God, and know my heart I pray.
Try me Oh Savior and see if there be some wicked
way in me.
Cleanse me from every sin and set me free.
(Words by J. Edwin Orr)

NOT ONE GOOD ONE

He who trusts in his own heart is a fool. But whoever walks wisely will be delivered.
(Proverbs 28:26)

Scripture clearly states there is **no one** who is good but God; NONE! All capital letters. That is why we have to keep our eyes on Jesus. When we start looking at others and putting them up on pedestals, we set ourselves up for disappointment. They are human just like we are. The only one that knew no sin is Christ.

THE DECEITFUL HEART

The heart is deceitful above all things, and desperately wicked; who can know it? I, the Lord, search the heart, I test the mind, even to give every man according to his ways, according to the fruit of his doings.
(Jeremiah 17:9-10)

The heart is our inner self which thinks, feels and acts. Oh, how we need the touch of the Master's hand to give us a "heart transplant"! All of our righteousness is like a filthy rag before Him.

> *For out of the heart proceed evil thoughts, mur-*
> *ders, adulterer's fornication, thefts, false witness,*
> *blasphemies.*
> (Matthew 15:19)

The heart is the source of ALL evil action. When we turn our hearts over to Christ, He offers promises to us in His Word:

> *Blessed are the pure in heart, for they shall see*
> *God.*
> (Matthew 5:8)

> *Then I will give them a heart to know Me, that I*
> *am the Lord; and they shall be My people and I*
> *will be their God, for they shall return to Me with*
> *their whole heart.*
> (Jeremiah 24:7)

> *Then I will give them one heart, and I will put a*
> *new spirit within them, and take the stony heart*
> *out of their flesh, and give them a heart of flesh.*
> (Ezekiel 11:19)

When we give our whole hearts to Christ, He does a "transformation" in our lives, both spiritually and morally.

SQUEAKY CLEAN

One of my favorite things to do is take a nice, long, hot bath. I like the water so hot that I can barely step in; adding in some bath salts, crystals, or anything to make bubbles is the ultimate experience. When my children were young, there was not much time to allow myself such a luxury.

JESUS' BUBBLE BATH

Sometimes I compare bathing to my spiritual life. My heart was dirty, then Jesus came in like an effervescent tablet bursting all the dirty pockets of sin and disintegrating them. Now it is clean.

Remember the old tablets we used to put in our mouths that turned our teeth pink and cleaned all the scum away? That is what Jesus did when the presence of the Holy Spirit shone its light into your dark heart and mine. He scrubbed us clean like all those bubble bath bubbles and we came out a new, sparkling-clean creation in His sight.

Jesus cleansed me and made me whole.

BABY FRESH

There is nothing like the smell and softness of a new baby. That is how we feel when Christ shines His love into our deceitful and sinful hearts. When we are baptized by His precious Holy Spirit, we feel "squeaky clean." It is a supernatural experience. It is nothing anyone can do for us except Christ. He alone can make us worthy through His blood.

Not only does Jesus cleanse us, but He softens our hearts. He adds a touch of gentleness like a fabric softener to smooth out those rough edges and make us more touchable. The difference is amazing! We hardly notice when others are not doing things exactly the way we want them to.

FULL OF DIRT AND GRIME

Another way to look at our hearts is like a dirty furnace filter. When you take the filter out to clean it, all of the little holes in the screen are completely blocked and full of dirt and grime. It looks impenetrable.

I can only imagine that is how our hearts look to Christ: black and ugly.

Aren't you thankful that Christ's love is able to penetrate even the darkest of sins? I know I am. There is nothing we have done that is too awful for God's tidal wave of love to come crashing over and completely wipe away. The Bible says He not only forgives, but He forgets too. He puts our sins as far away from the East is from the West.

DEEPER THAN THE DEEPEST OCEAN

Praise God for His amazing love and forgiveness! It is deeper than the deepest ocean and higher than the highest heavens. It was there before we were born and will be there the day we die. When you cannot count on anything else, you can count on God's amazing grace and forgiveness.

Have you been washed in the cleansing fountain of God's grace? Let Him give you a bubble bath in the Holy Spirit and wash you whiter than snow. I promise you it will be the ultimate "spa experience."

Purge me with hyssop, and I shall be clean; wash me, and I shall be whiter than snow.

(Psalm 51:7)

Create in me a clean heart, O God, and renew a steadfast spirit within me.

(Psalm 51:10)

FORGIVENESS

For me, this will probably be the hardest part of my writing. Not because I have a hard time forgiving, but because of the enormous amount of pain that has come with it. I am so thankful for the unconditional pardon the Father has bestowed upon me so that I am also able to forgive others!

In Him we have redemption through His blood, the forgiveness of sins according to the riches of His grace.

(Ephesians 1:7)

THANK YOU, JESUS!

The grounds of all grace come from the reconciling death of Jesus on the cross. At the expense of His redeeming blood alone, God offers forgiveness.

Forgiveness is made possible because Christ loved us so much. I am reminded of the song that says:

> *When I think about His love,*
> *How He saved me,*
> *How He forgave me,*
> *How He filled me with the Holy Ghost,*
> *How He saved me to the uttermost,*

41

It makes me want to shout, HALLELUJAH!
Thank you, Jesus for all You've done for me.
(Words by James Huey)

CLINGING DESPERATELY TO FAITH

My childhood was anything but ideal. I suffered both physically and emotionally at the hand of someone close to me, resulting in many nightmares, even into my adult life. Obviously I find it hard to say "I love you" to a person who has hurt me so deeply. It has truly been a lifetime of healing for me.

I gave my heart to Jesus as a young girl and I clung to my faith desperately during those times.

One day, as an adult, I laid it all down at the feet of Jesus – all the hurts, all the pain and disappointments, and it seemed I cried for hours. The pain was so real, so intense, so heavy.

After I gave it ALL to Jesus that day, He filled me with incredible joy. I began laughing in the Holy Spirit and the presence of God was so real that I just wanted to stay there and never get up.

God is so good! His mercies endure forever and His love is deeper than the deepest ocean.

GOD'S GRACE IS SUFFICIENT

I called this certain person, and told them that I loved them in spite of everything and that I forgave them. It was not easy to do, but I knew I needed to do it and God's grace was sufficient to help me.

Did you know God will never ask you to forgive another person more than He has already forgiven you?

My pastor has taught me many truths about forgiveness. He said that sometimes in our lives, we will need to be forgiven and we will not be able to receive what we are unwilling to give ourselves.

> *For if you forgive men their trespasses, your heavenly Father will also forgive you. But if you do not forgive men their trespasses, neither will your Father forgive your trespasses.*
> (Matthew 6:14-15)

When we think about how freely God has forgiven us, we know we should practice forgiveness to others. Sometimes it is easy to forget how gracious God has been to us. Unfortunately, our natural pettiness of heart and soul breed unforgiveness.

Restoration through the Grace of God

Over the years, my relationship with that particular person is being restored little by little. This restoration is only possible through God's amazing grace. If it were not for that grace, forgiveness and love would be replaced with bitterness and hate.

God is able to do the impossible. He is able to take a stony heart of clay and remake it into something beautiful. Doesn't that make you glad?

Nothing is impossible with God; He can do abundantly above anything we could ever ask or hope for. Praise His name forever!

A ROAD BLOCK TO RELATIONSHIP

"Cease from anger and forsake wrath; do not fret – it only causes harm" (Psalm 37:8). Did you know resentment is destructive? It is a road block to our relationship with God. My pastor has taught us that revenge will do more harm to us than to others when we harbor it, and bitterness depletes emotional energy and leads to depression and a miserable life. He also teaches us that forgiveness is not an option; it is a part of the Christian life:

> *If we confess our sins, He is faithful and just to forgive us our sins and to cleanse us from all unrighteousness.*
>
> (1 John 1:9)

Jesus says of the woman who washed His feet with her tears and wiped them dry with her hair that her love resulted from her forgiveness; she realized how great her sins were.

Colossians 3:13 reminds us that we must make allowances for each other's faults. Remember the Lord forgave you, so you must forgive the person who offends you.

> *He will not always strive with us, nor will He keep His anger forever. He has not dealt with us according to our sins, nor punished us according to our iniquities. For as the heavens are high above the earth, so great is His mercy toward those who fear Him; as far as the east is from the*

*west, so far has He removed our transgressions
from us.*

(Psalm 103:9-12)

THE LIGHTHOUSE

Recently my husband and I purchased a large old cabin
cruiser that we are refurbishing. Last night we were sitting
in it in the midst of a bad storm. As the winds were howl-
ing, the water was rough, and lightening was flashing, I
began to reflect on my life.

THE STORMS OF LIFE

Have you ever noticed how much easier it is to *talk*
about praising God through the good and the bad than to *do
it* when you are actually experiencing a "storm" of your
own? Lately my family has been enduring several storms at
once, and the "ship" of my life has been bouncing up and
down, tossed to and fro while the winds howl and the seas
of my life are torn at and thrown around.

It is during these times that we need to "anchor" our
souls into God's Word, looking steadfastly to Jesus, the
"Lighthouse," and He will safely set us back on course and
help us to ride out the storm.

RECOGNIZING GOD'S HAND

Sometimes it is only when we come through the storm
and are back on shore that we can recognize the guidance
of the Father's hand and praise Him for His divine protec-

tion. But we would do best to praise Him in the midst of it; to turn our rudder FIRST toward Him when our "ship" is out to sea and we feel hopeless and alone.

Jesus said He will NEVER leave us or forsake us, and His Word is true. He is with me always and I am so thankful for that reality.

I am reminded of a song my parents used to sing about the old lighthouse:

> *There's a light on the hillside that overlooks life's sea.*
>
> *And when I'm tossed it sends a light that I might clearly see.*
>
> *And the light that shines in darkness will safely lead me home.*
>
> *If it wasn't for the Lighthouse, my ship would be no more.*
>
> *I thank God for the Lighthouse, I owe my life to Him,*
>
> *for Jesus is the Lighthouse and from the rocks of sin,*
>
> *He has shone His light around me, that I might clearly see,*
>
> *If it wasn't for the Lighthouse, tell me where would this ship be?*

(Words by R. Hinson)

SMOOTH SAILING

I know it will not always be smooth sailing, but I would not want to cruise through life any other way than having Christ as the captain of my "ship."

If you do not know Jesus as your captain, why not come on board today and ask Him to steer your life? Storms will come and tempests will rise, but the Word of the Lord is true and He will bring you to the other side when you trust in Him.

He calms the storm, so that its waves are still.
(Psalm 107:29)

And there will be a tabernacle for shade in the daytime from the heat, for a place of refuge, and for a shelter from storm and rain.
(Isaiah 4:6)

INNER TUBES

IN TUNE WITH OUR SURROUNDINGS

When my youngest daughter, Sarah, and I went to Cancun on her senior trip, we enjoyed floating down the river on an inner tube. It was so peaceful! We could hear the sounds of the birds and the other animals near by; we were in tune with our surroundings.

I wonder what the "inner tubes" of our hearts look like. Are they plugged with malice, hate, blackness and evil desires? Or are we in tune with God's Word and listening to His voice and His will for our life? As we travel through

47

each day, do we stop to listen to the voices around us?

I loved the book, *The Heart Reader*, about a man who was so in tune with those around him that he could hear the cries of their hearts. He could not get away from those cries because God had allowed him to be sensitized to the needs around him.

CAPTAIN JESUS

What kind of river are you floating down? Is it a dark, turbulent ride on the rapids, dodging rock boulders along the way? Or are you sailing through life with Jesus on board?

Is Jesus the captain of your life?

If the "tube" you are in is starting to deflate, there is One who can breathe the breath of life back into it. You do not have to struggle alone — reach out an oar to Jesus and He will grab it. You will be in for the ride of your life with the Savior. The storms of life will come, but never again will you ride them alone.

> *God is our refuge and strength, a very present help in trouble.*
>
> (Psalm 46:1)

> *...I am with you always, even to the end of the age.*
>
> (Matthew 28:20)

My mother used to sing a song called "Sheltered in the Arms of God" which contained a beautiful truth:

> *So let the storms rage high, the dark clouds rise.*

48

They won't worry me
for I'm sheltered safe within the arms of God.
He walks with me and naught of earth shall harm me,
for I'm sheltered in the arms of God.
(Words by Dottie Rambo & Jimmie Davis)

THE CLOTHESLINE

Ironing has always been my least favorite household chore. I would rather clean toilets! But for some reason this morning, when I was ironing, I began to think about laundry and my life.

WRINKLED AND OUT OF SORTS

I am so thankful that Jesus keeps working on me when I am wrinkled and all out of sorts. He applies a little starch and steams me right back into shape. When I come to Him dirty and unclean, He spot-treats me and washes me whiter than snow.

Sometimes, when my attitude is bad, I may need to be hung on the line to dry and bask in the sunshine of His light until once again I am fresh and renewed. When I really mess up, a little bleach may need to be applied to get out the really stubborn stains, and perhaps a touch of softener thrown in to add gentleness.

God is so good. We can see Him in everything we do if we just take time to bask in His love every day. The next time you carry a basketful of laundry, think about how God works to "sort out" the pieces of our lives and turns them into a beautiful wardrobe for His Kingdom.

A Beautiful Wardrobe

Speaking of wardrobes, that is what God's armor of protection is to us. Ephesians 6:14-17 tells us:

Stand therefore, having girded your waist with truth, having put on the breastplate of righteousness, and having shod your feet with the preparation of the gospel of peace; above all, taking the shield of faith with you which you will be able to quench ALL the fiery darts of the wicked one. And take the helmet of salvation, and the sword of the Spirit, which is the Word of God.

Just as we put on our natural clothing, we must put on the armor of God. Have you clothed yourself in God's armor? Put the pieces on every day and claim them through your relationship with Christ. Make it a daily habit.

We are no match for the enemy who is always lurking like a roaming lion seeking whom he may devour. We need every piece of God's armor to resist the enemy when he attacks us, or we will be vulnerable.

Big and Small

Each day, come before the Father and ask Him to help you in the small and big issues of your life. He is ready and waiting. Put on your armor and speak out against lies and temptations Satan may speak to your mind. Rebuke him in the name of Jesus and put him under your feet. God has given us that authority. Never give up. Thank the Father for who He is and who you are in Him.

Continue to clothe me, Lord, in Your wardrobe of righteousness and peace, and gird me about with all of Your armor.

THE WINDMILL

A windmill, according to the *American Heritage Dictionary*, is: a machine that runs on the energy generated by a wheel of adjustable blades or slats rotated by the wind. There is a windmill on top of a hill out on the old family farm that we purchased from my mother-in-law after my father-in-law died.

POWER UNLEASHED

I was thinking about the Holy Spirit and the power that is unleashed by a humble and contrite spirit, by a yielded life and an offering of sacrifice each day.

The possibilities are endless when we "tap into" God's source of power. Prayer is the key to unlocking that power. It is something so available to each of us, but so often unused.

When a storm hits and our power goes out, we scramble around trying to find candles and flashlights and are often in a state of frenzy until everything is restored.

THE POWER OF PRAYER

That is how it is in our spiritual lives as well. When the storms hit and we lose our way, and the lights go dark in our souls and spirits, we often reach out for everything else to restore us instead of the actual source of power. If only we would just "tap into" our most precious commodity: the power of prayer! We do not need a "back-up generator" to keep things running smoothly. God's Word says,

> *Your Word is a lamp unto my feet and a light to my path.*
>
> (Psalm 119:105)

Father, help turn on the "light bulb" in each of our lives to illuminate Your precious Word so that we might not sin against You.

JOY UNSPEAKABLE

Where would we be without joy? What kind of life would we have? Dead and dry.

BUBBLING UP FROM THE DEPTHS

Sometimes we take joy for granted, that wonderful feeling that comes bubbling up from the depths of our souls and into our spirits like a large jar of bubbles that you can blow and release into the air. Joy is the feeling we get when we want to dance before the Lord and shout and sing of His wonderful goodness to us; joy unspeakable and full of glory.

Joy is one of the fruits of the Spirit. It is a blessing from God. *"But the fruit of the Spirit is love, joy, peace, longsuffering, kindness, goodness, faithfulness, gentleness, self-control. Against such there is no law"* (Galatians 5:22-23).

As long as I have breath in my body, may I have a spirit of joy for all Christ has done for me!

PEACE AND JOY

Christ wants us to have peace in our lives, and He wants us to have joy.

Now may the God of hope fill you with all joy and peace in believing, that you may abound in hope by the power of the Holy Spirit.
(Romans 15:13)

Your words were found, and I ate them. And Your word was to me the joy and rejoicing of my heart; for I am called by Your name, O Lord God of hosts.
(Jeremiah 15:16)

You will show me the path of life; in Your presence is fullness of joy; at Your right hand are pleasures forevermore.
(Psalm 16:11)

And my soul shall be joyful in the Lord; it shall rejoice in His salvation.
(Psalm 35:9)

These things I have spoken to you, that My joy may remain in you, and that your joy may be full.
(John 15:11)

Thank You Lord, for Your unspeakable joy and glory that reach way down into the depths of my soul like a fountain of water, flowing into every part of my being.

Nothing, no circumstances, can take it away from me.

You are the giver of joy.

CHAPTER THREE

Attaining His Character

The character of Christ – what a lofty goal!
Thank You, Father, that the trials I endure serve
to make me more like Him!

FRIEND

It is an amazing truth to know that we can be called a friend of God. What a privilege!

HEALTHY FRIENDSHIPS

The word "friend" is described in the Spirit-Filled Life New King James version Bible as "Companion, neighbor, fellowman; a familiar person." Its root is the verb "ra'ah," which means "associate with, to be a friend of."

"A friend loveth at all times..." (Proverbs 17:17, KJV) – a prescription for a healthy friendship. How many friends do you have that love you all the time?

Do they love you when you disappoint them, when you let them down or use an angry tone?

Do they love you when you neglect them, ignore them, or when you are late?

At various times in our life we do all of these things to Christ, but He still loves us.

A man who has friends must himself be friendly, but there is a friend who sticks closer than a brother.

(Proverbs 18:24)

THE FAMILY OF CHRIST

Some of you may not have a good family structure. Maybe you are singled out in your family if you are a Christian.

Always know, however, when you are a friend of God, you belong to His family, the body of believers, and you never have to be alone.

And the Scripture was fulfilled which says, 'Abraham believed God, and it was accounted to him for righteousness.' And he was called the friend of God.

(James 2:23)

I have a special friend who is my "sister in Christ." We have been prayer partners for years now, and even though our physical locations are different, our spiritual ones are the same. We know at any time we can call on each other to join in prayer over any situation. God's Word tells us that where two or more are gathered He is in the midst of us.

Thank you, Wendy, for being a dear "sister and friend" in Christ.

Greater love has no one than this, than to lay down one's life for his friends.

(John 15:13)

This reminds me of the song:

> *Such love, such wondrous love,*
> *such love, such wondrous love*
> *that God would love a sinner such as I.*

(Words by C. Bishop)

How wonderful is love like this!

I hope you know the peace and joy of being called a friend of God. If not, why don't you ask Him to come into your heart and life today?

UNTITLED POEM

Blow some wind upon the flame
Oh God that burns within my heart
And let it shine ablaze for You
That I may do my part.

Lord let me carry burdens here
For souls lost everywhere
Let me feel deep sorrow for those
Lost in despair

But most of all a life to give to Thee
Mine, full of Thy shining love and glory
We have but one to give
I give my all to Thee

Let me be like a candle
That shines so bright for Thee
A light so small yet carries all
Thy love and kind mercy

A burden to bear, a heart in despair
Yet a light to show Your way
Flicker in me – set a fire free
That I may give my all to Thee.

*poem by author as a teenager

PRISMS

When I think of the word "prism," I think of a reflection of light. We used to have a big chandelier in our dining room above the table with lots of shimmering prisms hanging down from it.

A SHIMMERING LIGHT

The word "prism" means something different to me today: it means a reflection of who I am when I look inside; what is reflected out through my eyes, my smiles, my pain; everything I am.

I want to be a shimmering light for Christ.

I want to sparkle for You, Lord. Just like the chandelier cleaner I used to spray on, make me shine and sparkle for You. Your Word says we are to be a light for You, to show Your love to a lost and dying world. Make me a reflection of who You are. There is not any greater desire in my life; there is no one else I would rather reflect. I want to be an extension of You, a prism in the network of Your chandelier (Your body), branching out to shine light and dispel darkness.

A THING OF BEAUTY

A chandelier is a thing of beauty. When you turn it on, it dispels the dark and sends out a beautiful light.

Lord, help me to shine brightly for You, a reflection of Your love, Your glory, Your grace. I want to be a prism for Jesus.

59

Let your light so shine before men, that they may see your good works and glorify your Father in Heaven.

(Matthew 5:16)

This is the message which we have heard from Him and declare to you, that God is light and in Him is no darkness at all.

(1 John 1:5)

If we say we have fellowship with Him, and walk in darkness, we lie and do not practice the truth. But if we walk in the light as He is in the light, we have fellowship with one another and the blood of Jesus Christ His Son cleanses us from all sin.

(1 John 1:6-7)

WORDS OF ENCOURAGEMENT

"I CARE ABOUT YOU"

Have you ever met someone whose face shows "words of encouragement" without saying a word? I have. Our worship leader, Cheryl, is like that. Her face radiates love and the words, "I care about you." I do not think she realizes the blessing she is to so many and the encouragement she has been to me personally as a sister in Christ. Even though I do not know her well, I know her heart. I feel her compassion and I bond with her because we share the same Jesus.

That is what we are to be about: every day offering our bodies as a living sacrifice to You afresh, Lord, to be used for Your glory, Your purpose, Your plan. It is not about us, it is ALL about You. Cheryl truly understands that. She points all the worship, all the praise, everything to You and she leads us into that Spirit of praise with her.

JUST A STEPPING STONE

This world is just a stepping stone from which we will pass, and our bodies are just a shell, a vessel to house God's Holy Spirit, with which to show Christ to a hurting world.

May I always share the hope that is in me with others! I want my life to be a living testimony to my family, my friends, wherever I go and whoever I meet.

I like the song that says:

> *Take my life Lord and make it Yours,*
> *Take my family Lord, and make them Yours,*
> *Take my heart Lord, and make it Yours,*
> *Take it all Lord, make it Yours.*
>
> (Words by Scott Underwood)

REAL PEOPLE

We need "real" people in this world. We do not have to look very far to find pretense and lies, cover up and deception; but truth, respect and honesty are what people are really looking for – someone they can trust and share their heart with. I want to be a "real" person and I hope you do too.

Let's start today by applying a "facial scrub" and "cleansing mask" and let our faces shine for Jesus.

...that I may be encouraged together with you by

the mutual faith both of you and me.

(Romans 1:12)

That their hearts may be encouraged, being knit together in love, attaining to all riches of the full assurance of understanding, to the knowledge of the mystery of God, both of the Father and of Christ.

(Colossians 2:2)

THE WORSHIPER

HEART OF WORSHIP

God is calling each of us to a true heart of worship. I know I am as guilty as the next person of coming into His house with many other things on my mind.

It is all about Him.

It is all about Him.

Maybe we should say that over and over before we ever come into the sanctuary. I think I will begin to do that.

I believe God is searching every heart up and down each aisle, looking for true worshipers. He is searching for those who will worship Him in spirit and in truth, who sing because they truly love Jesus, not just because the words of the song say so. He is looking for those who will lift their hands because they sincerely want to worship and give honor to the Lord for all He has done in their lives, who will bow down in humility before an Almighty God who alone is worthy. He wants those who are not there merely to play church or be entertained.

62

Down on Our Knees

God is looking for a people to bow down and worship Him, to exalt and lift Him on high, to give honor and glory to an all-knowing, all-powerful, all-loving God who gave His only Son to die that they might have life. That act alone should be enough to cause each of us to get on our knees and cry out to the Father for forgiveness.

I know it makes me cry to think of how short I have fallen so many times.

I want to be a true worshipper. Lord, help me to leave all the stuff of my life outside the door of the sanctuary and to instead bring in the sacrifices of praise.

> *For it is written: 'As I live, says the Lord, every knee shall bow to Me, and every tongue shall confess to God.*
>
> (Romans 14:11)
>
> *For all have sinned and fall short of the glory of God.*
>
> (Romans 3:23)

The Color of Your Mood

What color are you in the morning light? Do your circumstances on the outside determine and reflect the color of your internal heart?

ANGELS ALL AROUND

God says there is nothing too difficult for Him. When the sunshine of our life turns to gray, God is still there. He goes before us and His angels protect us everywhere we go; they hold tightly to our hands. My daughter, Paige, used to sing a song in church about angels:

> *They're all above me, beneath me, before me, they're all around me;*

> *My Father's angels all protect me everywhere.*

> *I can never stray so far that my Father would lose track of where I am.*

> *Angels walk beside me, holding tightly to my hand.*

> *Even when the night is dark, I just can't see a thing in front of me;*

> *I don't need to worry; they can see. They can see me.*
>
> -(Words by, Gloria Gaither)

That is such a beautiful song, and a beautiful truth.

THE LIGHT OF JESUS' LOVE

When your heart is dark, you need the light of Jesus' love to shine in.

I like to think of my heart as pink, like a Pepto Bismol tablet that helps to soothe; or maybe yellow and sunny, bright and cheery, to spread warmth to those around me.

64

Even when it is hurt and crying I pray that it would radiate love. I want the color of my heart to be happy, forgiving, rejoicing, thankful, and most of all, loving.

Color my heart to reflect You, Lord.

I do not know what tomorrow may hold, but I know Who holds tomorrow and I know Who holds my hand. When the skies of my life seem to be falling, I know You will once again line them with a silver lining!

Oh, let the wickedness of the wicked come to an end, but establish the just; for the righteous God tests the hearts and minds.

(Psalm 7:9)

The humble shall see this and be glad; and you who seek God, your hearts shall live.

(Psalm 69:32)

...and the peace of God, which surpasses all understanding, will guard your hearts and minds through Christ Jesus.

(Philippians 4:7)

Glory in His holy name; let the hearts of those rejoice who seek the Lord.

(Psalm 105:3)

OPEN VALVE

Be anxious for nothing, but in everything by prayer and supplication, with thanksgiving, let your requests be made known to God; and the peace of God, which surpasses all understanding, will guard your hearts and minds through Christ Jesus.

(Philippians 4:6-7)

I think Jesus wants us to have an "open valve" in our hearts, open and running free with His good message to all those in our lives; not tightly shut off with our own views, hard-hearted and indifferent to those who do not believe as we do.

SAVE A SOUL

Let him know that he who turns a sinner from the error of his way will save a soul from death and cover a multitude of sins.

(James 5:20)

We need to live our life like an open valve, so others can see what is truly inside us, that our sins have been covered by the blood of Christ. Perhaps one day they too can come to know and love the same Jesus that we do.

Therefore lay aside all filthiness and overflow of wickedness, and receive with meekness the implanted word, which is able to save your souls.

(James 1:21)

How else can they see? How else can they learn of God's great love?

These thoughts bring me to my son, Eric. He has a brilliant mind and many talents. I love him and treasure his life. I continue to let my love flow out to him through the fountain Christ has poured into my life so that he may one day come to know the Father. He and I are friends and we love and appreciate each other, but my heart yearns for him to know the Savior and for his life to be complete.

Do Not Give up

Now may the God of peace Himself sanctify you completely; and may your whole spirit, soul and body be preserved blameless at the coming of our Lord Jesus Christ.

(1 Thessalonians 5:23)

Beloved, I pray that you may prosper in all things and be in health, just as your soul prospers.

(3 John 1:2)

Is there anyone in your life for whom you are praying these same prayers? I am sure there are.

Do not give up.

Keep believing and trusting God to cover you with His precious blood and to use you to pour His love through your "open valve" to a hurt and lost world.

And a servant of the Lord must not quarrel but be gentle to all, able to teach, patient, in humility correcting those who are in opposition, if God perhaps will grant them repentance, so that they may know the truth, and that they may come to their senses and escape the snare of the devil, having been taken captive by him to do his will.

(2 Timothy 2:24-26)

Unsung Angels

I received a card on Mother's Day this year from my daughter, Sarah, that spoke about unsung angels. I am not sure I live up to the title, but in my daughter's eyes I do. It sure made me feel good to know she thinks of me in that way.

67

A Beautiful Offering

I do want to fulfill the description on the card: someone who is willing to give of themselves and let their life be an offering to others. What a testimony of God's love and grace! I know I have many shortcomings and many faults, but I hope my children can see the better part of me, the part that exists because Christ is alive and working in my heart. He makes a beautiful offering out of my life. Without Him I am nothing.

When I think of the term "unsung angel," my mind paints a picture of an unselfish person: someone who is content to work in the shadows, who does not need the applause of others. I think of one who loves others unconditionally and looks past hurt and disappointments.

Spread Your Wings and Fly

Sometimes it can be a difficult job, but God supplies the grace, the tears, the joys and the forgiveness – everything we need for the job. He fully equips us to spread our "wings" and fly. If He calls us, He supplies us. All He asks is that we let Him guide our lives, and He will shelter us in His amazing wings of grace.

> *He who dwells in the secret place of the Most High shall abide under the shadow of the Almighty. I will say of the Lord, 'He is my refuge and my fortress; My God, in Him I will trust'.*
> (Psalm 91:1-2)

I believe angels must be very strong, but I also believe they are gentle spirits. I am so thankful every day for the guardian angels that watch over me and my loved ones.

...the unfading beauty of a gentle and quiet spir-it, which is of great worth in God's sight.
(1 Peter 3:4, NIV)

Let your gentleness be known to all men...
(Philippians 4:5)

Take My yoke upon you and learn from Me, for I am gentle and lowly in heart, and you will find rest for your souls.
(Matthew 11:29)

PURSUE GENTLENESS

What is the definition of gentleness? It certainly does not mean weakness. It is a disposition that is even-tempered, tranquil, balanced in spirit, unpretentious, and that has the passions under control.

Scripture tells us we are to pursue gentleness:

...pursue righteousness, godliness, faith, love, patience, gentleness.
(1 Timothy 6:11)

To speak evil of no one, to be peaceable, gentle, showing all humility to all men.
(Titus 3:2)

With all lowliness and gentleness, with longsuf-fering, bearing with one another in love.
(Ephesians 4:2)

But the fruit of the Spirit is love, joy, peace, long-suffering, kindness, goodness and faithfulness , gentleness, self-control. Against such there is no law.
(Galatians 5:22-23)

69

TENDER MERCIES

I believe God has called us to be compassionate.

But whoever has this world's goods, and sees his brother in need, and shuts up his heart from him, how does the love of God abide in him?

(1 John 3:17)

IT'S ALL YOURS

I want to hold loosely to the things of and in this world. I want to have a generous heart and share with those around me.

I believe one of the first words children learn is "mine."

Lord, help me not to be like a stingy child holding onto my "toys," unwilling to share with others.

Help us as adults to realize that everything belongs to You, Lord, and to be thankful for each blessing. I am grateful for the love and compassion You had for me when I was in the world and not living for You.

Should you not also have had compassion on your fellow servant, just as I had pity on you?

(Matthew 18:33)

But He, being full of compassion, forgave their iniquity, and did not destroy them. Yes, many a time He turned His anger away, and did not stir up all His wrath; for He remembered that they were but flesh, a breath that passes away and does not come again.

(Psalm 78:38-39)

But You, O Lord, are a God full of compassion, and gracious, longsuffering and abundant in mercy and truth.

(Psalm 86:15)

Through the Lord's mercies we are not consumed, because His compassions fail not.

(Lamentations 3:22)

Finally, all of you be of one mind, having compassion for one another; love as brothers, be tenderhearted, be courteous; not returning evil for evil or reviling for reviling, but on the contrary blessing, knowing that you were called to this, that you may inherit a blessing.

(1 Peter 3:8-9)

TALENTS

Have you ever met someone who is very gifted in many areas? My son Eric is like that. He was 13 years old when my husband and I married. I remember one of the first things he showed me was a poem he had written about Christmas. I was so impressed with his writing talent! Eric can also play several instruments without ever having taken a lesson, is a whiz on the computer, and has such a gift for drawing. He has a lot of talents wrapped up in one person!

USE IT WISELY

I am reminded of a story in the Bible where God speaks of talents in a different way. In the parable, the master divided out different talents or sums of money among his servants to see what they would do with what he gave. Some put it to work for his kingdom, and he was pleased with them. But one servant held on to his talent and did nothing to further the kingdom. The master was very displeased with him and cast him out.

This parable is speaking to us about how we live our lives. What are we doing for Christ? Sometimes it is in tangible ways that we bless others and sometimes it is just being there to listen, to speak kind words or to visit someone. It is all about ministering to someone else.

INHERIT THE KINGDOM

Some of us may feel like we do not have many "talents" or gifts. But God has given to each of us ways to bless others. If nothing else, we can always pray.

I want to hear Jesus say to me what He said in Matthew 25:34-36:

> *Come, you blessed of My Father, inherit the Kingdom prepared for you from the foundation of the world: for I was hungry and you gave Me food; I was thirsty and you gave Me a drink; I was a stranger and you took Me in; I was naked and you clothed Me; I was sick and you visited Me; I was in prison and you came to Me.*

When they asked Christ when this was that they had ministered to Him, He replied in verse 40,

> *...Assuredly, I say to you, inasmuch as you did it to one of the least of these My brethren, you did it to Me.*

What are we doing with the "talents" Christ has given to us?

May we examine our hearts before Him and make sure we are living our life so that it is a sweet-smelling sacrifice to others!

INSIDE OUT

OUR TRUE CHARACTER

Have you ever heard the song: "What goes up must come down"? I believe that principle also works in a different way. The things we feed our minds and hearts with will surely come out in our lives and show our true character.

Lord, my heart is not haughty, nor my eyes lofty. Neither do I concern myself with great matters, nor with things too profound for me.

(Psalm 131:1)

The description Jesus gave of Himself was "gentle and lowly in heart; humble."

Oh, to be like Jesus, all I ask is to be like Him! I pray that I could learn to quiet my heart and spirit before an awesome and loving God; to learn His nature and truly be like Him.

WHAT DO YOU EAT?

"For as he thinks in his heart, so is he..." (Proverbs 23:7). This is speaking of the things we digest and feed our minds and souls on; they will surely reflect who we really are. How

careful we should be to hide God's Word in our hearts and to be ready every day to give an answer to others of the hope that is in us to a lost and hurting world!

What would we look like if we turned ourselves inside out? I shudder to think of it. What if what everyone saw was not our physical appearance, but our "heart" appearance? The things we keep hidden would be exposed, the feelings, the pride, the evil thoughts and desires.

YOU CAN'T HIDE

Jesus sees it all; we cannot hide from Him. He loves us and desires for us to be new creatures.

> *By humility and the fear of the Lord are riches and honor and life.*
> (Proverbs 22:4)

The definition of humility as used in Acts 20:19 is "modesty, lowliness, humble-mindedness, a sense of moral insignificance and a humble attitude of unselfish concern for the welfare of others, a total absence of arrogance, conceit and haughtiness."

Scripture tells us that we are to be *"clothed with humility, for God resists the proud, but gives grace to the humble."* Therefore, we are to humble ourselves under the mighty hand of God, that He may exalt us in due time (1 Peter 5:5-6). Christ is not coming back for a proud and haughty bride. He is coming back for one with a gentle spirit that models His character.

"To speak evil of no one, to be peaceable, gentle, showing all humility to all men" (Titus 3:2). This means we are

74

responsible for our actions to everyone, people inside and outside the body of believers. We are to be kind and gentle that we may influence those around us for good.

CROWDED ROOMS

SPRING CLEANING

Just like the rooms in our home need spring cleaning, so do the rooms in our heart. They get cluttered with a lot of unnecessary "stuff" and we need to get the spiritual "broom" out and sweep away some of the dirt and excess baggage that can so easily weigh us down.

The older I get the more I realize the less I need. I think we spend far too much time trying to acquire and acquire, to fill every space in our home and in our hearts.

Let's clean it out and have a garage sale!

Are there some things you can part with? I bet there are, just as there are in my life.

THE MASTER'S SUITE

Sometimes we fill our rooms with good things like charitable items, but are we leaving room for Christ? His room in our heart should be the master suite, taking up the largest part; then the rest of the layout will work out just fine.

I love that old song:

There's room at the cross for you,

75

There's room at the cross for you.
Though millions have come,
There is still room for one,
There's room at the cross for you.
(Words by Ira F. Stanphill)

"Little children, keep yourselves from idols..." (1 John 5:21). In other words, we need to keep away from anything that may take God's place in our hearts.

Are we making room for Christ? He has made room for us at the cross.

But God demonstrates His own love toward us, in that while we were still sinners, Christ died for us.
(Romans 5:8)

TIME OUT

If you have ever had or been around children you are probably familiar with a phrase called "time out." What purpose does a time out really serve? It helps children to focus on getting still, collecting their thoughts and behavior, and composing themselves to carry on in their play or chores.

BE QUIET

I think sometimes as adults we also need "time out" in order to discipline ourselves to be quiet before an Almighty God, to seek His will and direction instead of our own, and to let Him refocus our priorities. Sometimes we get so busy with our work and play that we forget to honor God and spend quality time with Him. He is worthy of the first part of every day.

Jesus Himself spent quiet time alone before God, seeking His will. What better example could we have than that?

I think "time out" is a very effective discipline structure for children, as it causes them to reflect on the consequences of their actions. I want to put it into practice more in my every day life. No matter how hectic my schedule may be, it will go smoother when we place everything in God's hands.

As the deer pants for the water brooks, so pants my soul for You, O God. My soul thirsts for God, for the living God...

(Psalm 42:1-2)

GOOD AND PLENTY

Remember the box of pink and white candy called "Good & Plenty"? I used to take every piece of candy out of the box and count them one by one.

Sometimes I think about how much "good and plenty" is evident in my life. What does it really mean to be good? The Bible says there is none good but God, and that ALL of our righteousness is like a filthy rag.

MORE THAN ENOUGH

I am sure many of you have heard the saying, "Every day is a gift." Every day *is* a gift; that is why it is called "the present." We only have so many seconds, minutes and hours in a day's time, and we use it up somehow. We need to come to the throne room of grace *every day* to ask Christ to refill us and make us more like Him.

The word "plenty" means more than enough, running over. Do we have more than enough of Jesus in our lives, so that it spills out to those around us?

Filled to the Brim with Jesus

I want to be like a box of Good & Plenty. I want to be counted as one who shares what they have with others. Even if my life gets shaken up, when it settles, may the goodness of Christ be on top of the whole pile. I want to overflow this package, this shell called a body, running over the top, totally sold out to Christ. I want my net weight to say "filled to the brim with Jesus."

What kind of candy represents your life? Are you like black licorice, hard and bitter and full of dark secrets and unforgiveness? Or are you more like gummy bears, soft and squishy, riding the fence, unable to make up your mind who you want to live for? How about sweet tarts? Do you have two sides to you; sometimes sweet and sometimes sour? Maybe you are like red hots, on fire for God all the way.

Next time you eat a piece of candy, think about your life and how you think it is represented to those around you. Think about your friends and how you would categorize them.

It's All Good

O my soul, you have said to the Lord, 'You are my Lord, my goodness is nothing apart from You.'
(Psalm 16:2)

Teach me to do Your will, for You are my God; Your Spirit is good...
(Psalm 143:10)

But the fruit of the Spirit is love, joy, peace, long-suffering, kindness, goodness, faithfulness...
(Galatians 5:22)

Oh, how great is Your goodness, which You have laid up for those who fear You, which You have prepared for those who trust in You...
(Psalm 31:19)

The eyes of the Lord are in every place, keeping watch on the evil and the good.
(Proverbs 15:3)

Let them do good, that they be rich in good works, ready to give, willing to share, storing up for themselves a good foundation for the time to come, that they may lay hold on eternal life.
(1 Timothy 6:18-19)

No one is good, but One, that is, God.
(Matthew 19:17)

But love your enemies, do good and lend, hoping for nothing in return; and your reward will be great, and you will be sons of the Most High. For He is kind to the unthankful and evil. Therefore, be merciful, just as your Father also is merciful.
(Luke 6:35-36)

79

This kind of love speaks volumes to a world that is used to another kind of love, the kind that demands something in return. This kind of love and goodness is only possible when we become transformed into God's likeness.

To love the unlovely, the desperate, the poor – what better example can we be to the transforming power of grace in our lives?

> *Do not be overcome by evil, but overcome evil with good.*
>
> (Romans 12:21)

> *For scarcely for a righteous man will one die; yet perhaps for a good man someone would even dare to die. But God demonstrates His own love toward us, in that while we were still sinners, Christ died for us.*
>
> (Romans 5:7-8)

CROSSROADS

When my husband's grandparents were alive, we would go visit them in Mineral City. There was a restaurant near some railroad tracks called "Crossroads." It was one of their favorite places to eat. Nothing fancy, but comfortable and they enjoyed it. It is one of our fond memories with them.

CONSEQUENCES FOR THE FUTURE

I was thinking about the crossroads in our lives. There are so many! Each of those crossroads holds consequences for the future that we do not often think about, especially when we are young. Some of the choices we make can alter our lives forever. There is no going back, just moving forward.

That is how it is with our relationship to Christ. We come to many crossroads in our decisions to follow or not to follow, to be ashamed of Christ or to be a witness for Him, to straddle the fence or just jump over and give all we have to Him.

God's Word says if we are ashamed of Him on this earth, that He will be ashamed of us in Heaven.

Maybe you try to keep a little bit of God in your pocket just in case you need Him, instead of living your life totally sold out to Christ. The Bible says if we are lukewarm that He will spit us out of His mouth. He wants *everything*; every part of us; not just a piece.

THE TRAIN BOUND FOR HEAVEN

Are you lying on that crossroad, weary and worn out from trying to do things your way? Satan would love nothing more than to run that train right over the top of you, destroying your life in the process. Let God pack up the pieces of your life so that you can pick up your suitcase and get on the train bound for Heaven.

> *For whoever is ashamed of Me and My words in this adulterous and sinful generation, of him the Son of Man also will be ashamed when He comes in the glory of His Father with the holy angels.*
> (Mark 8:38)

WHERE IS YOUR CASTLE?

When you picture a castle, what do you see? Close your eyes and think about it.

Sometimes I picture the castle I once saw at Disney World. I remember how disappointed I was that you just walk right through the middle of it.

THE TREASURE OF YOUR HEART

God's Word says in Matthew 6:21, *"For where your treasure is, there your heart will be also."* We need to set our sights above. This world is not our home; we are just passing through. Jesus is our King and we are the daughters of the Most High. He is preparing a mansion for us in glory that will outshine any castle or mansion built on this earth.

Some years ago, my husband and I took a trip to London, England where we visited many beautiful castles and cathedrals. God's Word says one day not one brick or stone will be left upon another. Everything in this life is temporary. We must keep our sights on things above.

What about the treasure of our hearts?

Do not lay up for yourselves treasures on earth where moth and rust decay and where thieves break in and steal; but lay up for yourselves treasure in heaven, where neither moth nor rust destroys and where thieves do not break in and steal. For where your treasure is, there your heart will be also.

(Matthew 6:19-21)

OUR FORTRESS AND DELIVERER

Who lives in the castle of your heart? Is Jesus on the throne?

It is important for Christ to reign first and foremost in our hearts and lives if we are going to produce fruit. Just as in a castle, Christ is our high tower of refuge.

I will love You, O Lord, my strength. The Lord is my rock and my fortress and my deliverer; my God, my strength in whom I will trust; my shield and the horn of my salvation, my stronghold.
(Psalm 18:1-2)

Lord, how I love You! You have done such tremendous things for me!

For You are my refuge, a high tower where my enemies can never reach me.

(Psalm 61:3)

The Lord is my fort where I can enter and be safe; no one can follow me in and slay me. He is a rugged mountain where I hide. He is my Savior, a rock where none can reach me; a tower of safety. He is my shield. He is like the strong horn of a mighty fighting bull.

LIFE MORE ABUNDANTLY

I love those words! Imagine: the Lord of Lords and King of Kings cares enough about me to save me, to rescue me, to fight for me. He is an awesome God!

The Lord has prepared the way for us to have life and have it more abundantly. All He asks is to reign victoriously in our hearts.

For it is the God who commanded light to shine out of darkness, who has shone in our hearts to give the light of the knowledge of the glory of God in the face of Jesus Christ. But we have this treasure in earthen vessels, that the excellence of the power may be of God and not of us.

(2 Corinthians 4:6-7)

I rejoice at Your word as one who finds great treasure.

(Psalm 119:162)

MARTHA'S WORLD

LEARNING TO WAIT

My daughter and son-in-law got me a book for Mother's Day this year, titled *Having a Mary's Heart in a Martha's World*. Boy, can I see myself in that book! It was a very good gift for me, as it is really speaking to me about the better part: learning to wait before Christ.

I am a busy-bee type, always moving and always doing. I love to serve my family and others and am usually multi-tasking whenever possible. However, one of the things I want to do is learn to let God lead; to take it down a notch, relax more and enjoy what God wants to say to me.

I need to learn to wait.

Waiting is something I have always struggled with. My brothers and I learned good work ethics at an early age. We had all kinds of animals to care for and large gardens that needed hoeing and weeding. If we were caught not doing our part, extra duties were added to our chore list, so we kept busy. "Keeping busy" has carried into each of our adult lives.

Hard work can be a good thing and the Bible teaches it is not good to be lazy or idle, but it is also very important to take time to wait on the Lord, to have a two-way conversation with Him and not just a one-way dialogue. We need to listen to what He wants to speak to our hearts.

Laziness casts one into a deep sleep, and an idle person will suffer hunger.
(Proverbs 19:15)

MY GOD WILL HEAR ME

Lord, help me in this area of my life! If there are other women out there struggling to wait before You, I pray You will help them as well.

Wait on the Lord; be of good courage, and He shall strengthen your heart; wait, I say, on the Lord.
(Psalm 27:14)

But those who wait on the Lord shall renew their strength; they shall mount up with wings like eagles, they shall run and not be weary, they shall walk and not faint.
(Isaiah 40:31)

Therefore, I will look to the Lord; I will wait for the God of my salvation; my God will hear me.
(Micah 7:7)

CHAPTER FOUR

Lessons From Nature

Oh, the beauty of creation!
To see it is to know the Creator Himself.

*"For since the creation of the world His invisible
attributes are clearly seen…"*

Oh Lord, may the glory of nature around me
remind me of Your glory!

LET THE SUNSHINE IN

Part of my high school years were spent in Stuart, Florida, where I had one teacher who for the entire year would pull down the shades every morning between classes and make the room dark. Then he would play the song, "Let the Sunshine in" and pull up the blinds. That memory has stuck with me all these years.

WALK IN THE LIGHT

Once we become Christians, the sunshine of God's love floods our souls and we need to show it to a dark and lost world. *"But if we walk in the light as He is in the light, we have fellowship with one another, and the blood of Jesus Christ His Son cleanses us from all sin"* (1 John 1:7).

Even when the skies of life turn gray and the thunder rolls and the lightening strikes, the storm cannot take away the sunshine that brings out the rainbow afterwards.

Jesus' light dispels darkness.

THE STORMS OF LIFE

Recently we had a terrible storm and the top of one of our large trees came over onto the house and put a hole in our roof. Water came in, damaging part of our ceiling and soaking part of our bedroom carpet, my quilt and several items of clothing in the closet.

Likewise, some of the things which are going to happen in life may not be very pleasant; but I am thankful that my joy does not depend on circumstances. Even when I am going through hard times, Christ's love still comes in and helps me to see the good through the bad.

For the Lord God is a sun and shield; the Lord bestows favor and honor; no good thing does He withhold from those whose walk is blameless.

(Psalm 84:11, NIV)

The Light of the World

We are to be the light of the world.

...let your light so shine before men, that they may see your good works and glorify your Father in heaven.

(Matthew 5:16)

Is the sunshine of God's love shining through your life? I know I want it to shine through mine.

Father, when others look at me, may they see Your love radiating through my actions, my eyes and my life.

Mud Bath

Wallowing in the Mud

Baby pigs are cute. In fact, I think they are adorable. When I was a young girl, I loved to hold and bottle-feed them and dress them up in doll clothes. But that cuteness does not last long. Soon, they are out there wallowing in the mud and loving it.

Sometimes that is what we Christians do. We turn our backs on Christ and wallow in the sins of the world jut like pigs. The good news is that Christ still loves us.

I met a good friend that I have had since school days, Sandra, while chasing pigs in her neighborhood. How embarrassing! My dad, my brothers and I were all trying to catch the pigs and bring them back to our farm. Sometimes I think about that day and how it brought me into relationships I have had for many years since. We laugh about it now, but it certainly was not funny then.

THROUGH THE MUCK AND MIRE

That is how it is with life. Looking back after coming through a situation is not nearly as painful as when we are going through the "muck and mire" of it. But I believe God uses the "mud bath" at different times in our lives so we can see more clearly when we wash it out of our eyes.

Life is not always sweet smelling and pretty, and how we deal with the "dirt" – the ugly situations, the painful remarks, the peer pressure, the misunderstandings – is what is important.

I know I have felt like the "prodigal daughter" more than once – walking in the ways of the world and taking a "mud bath" in sin. I am so thankful that God kept His hand upon my life, pulling me back to the shower of fresh living water; out of the pigpen and into His glorious Kingdom.

Sometimes we have to stand before God and let Him give a "detoxification" bath to not only our bodies, but to our hearts, souls and spirits in order to cleanse us from all the filth we put in there. It is a painful, but necessary experience.

91

Just like the song says:

Search me, oh God and know my heart today,
try me, oh Savior, know my thoughts I pray.
See if there be some wicked way in me,
cleanse me from every sin and set me free.

(Words by J. Edwin Orr)

ROOTS

We have a very large yard with many old trees. One year we replaced our old brick sidewalk with stamped concrete, and edged our driveway and landscaping with colored decorative concrete. Within the next year the concrete began to have cracks in it as the large tree roots caused it to rise and it began to crumble.

DEEP ROOTS

Roots go very deep. That is how we want the Word of God to run in our lives; deep. We want to saturate ourselves in it and become "rooted and grounded" in the truth, so when Satan's temptations come along (and they will), we are anchored on solid ground just like those old trees.

I love that song:

Just like a tree planted by the water,
I shall not be moved.

(Words by Sandra T. Ford)

As you therefore have received Christ Jesus the Lord, so walk in Him, rooted and built up in Him

92

*and established in the faith, as you have been
taught, abounding in it with thanksgiving.*
(Colossians 2:6-7)

*That Christ may dwell in your hearts through
faith; that you, being rooted and grounded in
love, may be able to comprehend with all the
saints what is the width and length and depth
and height – to know the love of Christ which
passes knowledge; that you may be filled with all
the fullness of God.*
(Ephesians 3:17-19)

*I, Jesus, have sent My angel to testify to you these
things in the churches. I am the Root and the Off-
spring of David, the Bright and Morning Star.*
(Revelation 22:16)

*Looking carefully lest anyone fall short of the
grace of God; lest any root of bitterness springing
up cause trouble, and by this many become
defiled.*
(Hebrews 12:15)

SHAKE OFF THE THINGS OF THE WORLD

As troubles and trials enter our lives, we must make
sure bitterness and strife do not get a hold of us. We have
to shake off the things of this world and not let them get
embedded into the soil of our lives. We must look to the
vine, which is Jesus, from which we receive our nourish-
ment for each day and our strength to stand strong when
the storms of life weather us and tear at our very being.

Christ is the Vine and we are the branches. When we
become "cut off" from His supply, our leaves wither and
turn dry; they blow away just like our joy.

93

But when we are connected to the Vine, our life flourishes and we "grow" buds and sprouts, and branch out to spread God's light to those under our cover.

Just like mature trees, we provide shade and shelter. Those aged trees may look old and twisted, but they are standing firm and cannot easily be shaken, even when the winds blow, the storms come and seasons change.

Help us, Lord, to be rooted and grounded in Your Word, Your truth and Your will. Amen.

HOW DOES YOUR GARDEN GROW?

Deep down in the very depths of our souls we water and fertilize that which dwells in our hearts.

How rich is the soil you are using to cultivate the treasures of your heart? Is it a nice, heavy mulch used to cover and protect your loved ones? Or is it a dry, prickly bale of straw loosely spread, way too thin?

SOWING TAKES TIME AND PATIENCE

Sowing takes time and patience: planting seeds, watering and waiting. More often than not, however, we want to see the results right away.

God's Word tells us to plant the seeds and let them sprout up in good time as they are cultivated and nourished.

God's Word is the seed we are to be planting.

Help it not to fall on deaf ears, Lord. Help me to water and care for all those You have placed in my garden of life, all those I brush shoulders with every day, everywhere I go. Help me to plant seeds of kindness, humility, forgiveness, generosity, joy, peace, gentleness, faith, patience...but most of all, seeds of love.

May I not get hasty with or lash out at, uproot or plow over the "plants" You have given me. May I use my hands to stake them up, to pat soil with good nutrients around their roots and to sprinkle them with showers of blessings. May I lovingly care for them as You do Your sheep.

FULL OF JOY FOR JESUS

I want to have a garden full of plants for You, Lord. May my garden shine bright like a field of sunflowers, full of joy for Jesus!

Think about your garden. How is it growing?

The Lord God planted a garden eastward in Eden, and there He put the man whom he had formed.

(Genesis 2:8)

The Lord will guide you continually, and satisfy your soul in drought, and strengthen your bones; you shall be like a watered garden, and like a spring of water, whose waters do not fail.

(Isaiah 58:11)

95

PLANTING SEEDS

The field is the world, the good seeds are the sons of the kingdom, but the tares are the sons of the wicked one.

(Matthew 13:38)

Have you ever planted a garden? You put that little seed in the ground, water and fertilize it, watch over it and pray for a good crop.

ANOTHER SOLDIER IN GOD'S ARMY

There is a similar scenario with our children's lives. We take those tiny new lives that God has entrusted into our care; we feed and nourish their bodies and spiritually nourish their minds and souls. We pray for and over them and watch them grow. We pray blessings into their lives and hope they will "sprout up," if you will, as a soul for Christ – another soldier in the field of God's army.

...having been born again, not of corruptible seed but incorruptible, through the Word of God which lives and abides forever.

(1 Peter 1:23)

THE RIGHT KIND OF SEEDS

Help us to plant seeds of forgiveness, love and peace into the lives of others, Lord!

The law of the Lord is perfect, converting the soul...

(Psalm 19:7)

96

He restores my soul; He leads me in the paths of righteousness for His name's sake.
(Psalm 23:3)

My soul shall make its boast in the Lord...
(Psalm 34:2)

Jesus said to him, 'You shall love the Lord your God with all your heart, with all your soul, and with all your mind.'
(Matthew 22:37)

Truly my soul silently waits for God...
(Psalm 62:1)

The fruit of the righteous is a tree of life, and he who wins souls is wise.
(Proverbs 11:30)

Let me be that kind of sower Lord, winning souls for Your Kingdom in the field of life."

Then He said to His disciples, 'The harvest truly is plentiful, but the laborers are few. Therefore, pray the Lord of the harvest to send out laborers into His harvest.'
(Matthew 9:37-38)

RESERVOIR

Reservoir: a natural or artificial pond or lake used for the storage and regulation of water.

We bought the family farm after my father-in-law passed away three years ago. My husband recently had work done to the spring that supplies the pond on the property. He is trying to create a fresh reservoir for fish and drinking water for animals.

NEVER THIRST AGAIN

I am reminded of the passage in John 4:14 when Jesus said,

...whoever drinks of the water that I shall give him will never thirst again. But the water that I shall give him will become in him a fountain of water springing up into everlasting life.

Do you sometimes feel like your heart is a dry and parched land instead of a spring of bubbling water? I know I do.

When our lives become spiritually stagnant the water turns murky and nothing is able to survive. When we are full of the "living water," however, it regenerates into everlasting life.

I want my springs of water to run fresh every day. Rain down on me, Lord; wash my heart and make it clean. Put a pure spirit within me.

WATCH OVER ONE ANOTHER

...looking carefully lest anyone fall short of the grace of God; lest any root of bitterness springing up cause trouble...

(Hebrews 12:15)

We are to watch over one another so that none leave the faith.

If we seek God with all of our hearts, He promises:

I will open rivers in desolate heights, and fountains in the midst of the valleys; I will make the wilderness a pool of water, and the dry land springs of water.

(Isaiah 41:18)

How much more does He desire for us to be drinking from the fountain of living water?

Does a spring send forth fresh water and bitter from the same opening?

(James 3:11)

James is referring to our tongues. We cannot be experiencing the streams of living water when what we say is not in line with God's will.

Wash me and I will be whiter than snow. Holy Spirit, rain down, rain down, rain down on me.

Jesus says,

...If anyone thirsts, let him come to Me and drink. He who believes in Me, as the Scripture has said, out of his heart will flow rivers of living water.

(John 7:37-38)

Is that the cry of your heart today?

Spirit of the Living God, fall fresh on me!

FLYING HIGH

My husband and I were in our boat on Salt Fork Lake one day when I observed an eagle soaring. It looked so effortless and carefree.

LAY DOWN YOUR BURDENS

That is how Christ wants us to be. He wants us to lay all our burdens down on His shoulders, at the foot of the cross, for He is more than able to handle anything that we bring to Him.

Sometimes we put them down for a brief time but then pick them right back up. I know I am guilty of that.

Continuing to carry our burdens is like struggling to hold a heavy backpack everywhere we go, filled with the weight of all our problems and those of others. Christ wants us to climb to the top of the prayer mountain and take that thing off of our backs. He said, "My yoke is easy and my burden is light."

FLY WITH CHRIST

I want to be lifted up like wings of eagles, to feel the air current of the Holy Spirit raising me up. I want to spread my holy hands to Christ and soar with Jesus; to breathe in the freshness of His Spirit until it fills my lungs and every part of me.

I want the ultimate high — to fly with Christ. No commercial airliner or private plane can compare to that. You do not need a pull-down oxygen mask or a flotation device if something goes wrong, just a willing heart and obedient spirit.

Let go and let Christ take the "wings" of your life. You may take a dip or even a nose dive, perhaps fall flat on your "beak." But, like the song says:

They that wait upon the Lord
shall renew their strength,
they shall mount up with wings like eagles,
they shall run and not be weary,
they shall walk and not faint,
teach me Lord, teach me Lord, how to wait.
(Words by Stuart Hamblen)

Waiting. That is not something I am good at. I am a get-to-it kind of girl, always moving, not much sitting. A two-hour plane ride and I am ready to disembark!

Lord, help me to wait before You, to bask in Your presence and learn to soar like the eagles.

Take My yoke upon you and learn from Me, for I am gentle and lowly in heart, and you will find rest for your souls. For My yoke is easy and My burden is light.
(Matthew 11:29-30)

CHAPTER FIVE

The Riches of Relationships

Thank You, Father, for those
You have carefully placed around me.
May love abound in us as it does in You!

Silk Petals

When I was a little girl, one of my bedrooms was all done in the color red. At that time, it was my favorite color. I had red carpet with light pink walls and red accessories. I just loved that cozy little room with the walls that slanted down!

Some of my fondest memories were coming home from school and finding a little gift from my mother on my cedar chest. It could have just been a dollar item; it did not matter. Just knowing how much my mother loved me was the best feeling. Her love was like a "silk petal" in my life.

It's the Little Things in Life

To me love is all about the small things; they all add up to become a beautiful bouquet. Each evening after my two brothers and I had our baths, we would settle down to watch television before bed and Mom would make us a special snack. My favorite was a bologna sandwich and chocolate ice cream. I still love bologna sandwiches to this day, and chocolate is my all-time favorite.

Looking back, I remember so many kindnesses Mom showed to me, and a lot of sacrifices. Her love is like a sweet-smelling bouquet of silky flowers. Like I said before, it has always been the simple things in life that give me the most pleasure.

Fond Memories

I remember when I was growing up, we lived on a farm and we had a small pond on the property. My brothers and

I used to ice skate until our fingers were numb and we thought for sure they would fall off from frost bite before we got back into the house. Mom would peel all the layers of clothing off and put them in the dryer while we thawed out and had a snack. Sure enough, we would put everything back on and head out to skate some more.

One of my fondest memories of the pond was lying down on the frozen water, trying to peer through the layers of ice to see the fish below. I would make snow angels and think of all the creatures below me.

My brothers and I had many wonderful winter days building snowmen and ice igloos, and riding sleds.

No Trading Here

I know you cannot choose your siblings, but even if I could, I would never want to trade mine in. We have been through a lot together and we have kindred hearts and spirits; the kind of relationship that says, "I will stand by you through the thick and the thin." Ray, Van and I are like best friends.

Best friends love you when you are down, when you are hurting and when your life is a mess, and they also rejoice with you in the great times.

Closer than a Sister

Best friends are hard to find. A best friend should not be jealous or envious and they should always point you to the Father in every situation.

I am thinking right now of one such friend, who was closer than a sister to me when I was going through my divorce. She showed me mercy though I am sure she got tired of seeing me, tired of listening. I depended on her love and care at that time more than she will ever know. She was showing Christ's love to me.

Thank you, Diane!

Even now, we may only see each other a few times a year, but she is in my thoughts and prayers, and our hearts have a special bond.

I also have to mention Diane's husband, Don. I have never forgotten your kindnesses to me either during such a difficult time in my life. I remember one night Sarah and I were staying at your house and Sarah was up crying in the middle of the night. I was afraid she would wake everyone up so I took her to the basement and was walking her around. Here you came with a rocking chair for me to use to rock her.

I have never forgotten it!

It may seem like a very small thing but to me it was a great act of kindness.

THE BEST OF FRIENDS

Where would we be without our very best friend, Jesus? The Bible says God sticketh closer than a brother or a sister. Even when He looks way down deep into our hearts, and they do not look very pretty, He still loves us. He is not a fair-weather friend.

In spite of the wickedness of mankind, Christ still loved us.

> *Then the Lord saw that the wickedness of man was very great in the earth, and that every intent of the thoughts of his heart was only evil continually.*
>
> (Genesis 6:5)

> *And Hannah prayed and said: 'My heart rejoices in the Lord; my horn [strength] is exalted in the Lord.'*
>
> (1 Samuel 2:1)

Hannah's whole personality was involved in praising the Lord.

LOOK AT THE HEART

I am so thankful that God does not look at physical beauty or appearance when He sees us, as we judge each other. Rather, the Lord looks at the heart (1 Samuel 16:7).

What does your heart yearn for?

Proverbs 31:30 says,

> *Charm is deceitful and beauty is passing, but a woman who fears the Lord, she shall be praised.*

I want to be that kind of woman: a woman like Hannah whose heart sought to please the Father, don't you? I want to praise my God in every situation, good or bad. He is the only one worthy of such praise and worship.

INWARD BEAUTY

*Do not let your adornment be merely outward —
arranging the hair, wearing gold, or putting on
fine apparel — rather let it be the hidden person
of the heart, with the incorruptible beauty of a
gentle and quiet spirit, which is very precious in
the sight of God.*

(1 Peter 3:3-4)

I want to be attractive to my husband; I am sure all of you ladies reading this want ot feel attractive, whether you are married or not. We want to feel beautiful and we want someone to notice us.

However, I do not want to merely have outward beauty with an inside that is rotten, ugly and decaying. I want my inside beauty to come forth and be displayed on the outside: a joyful smile, eyes that say I care along with the humility of knowing it is all about HIM; a beauty that says, "I belong to the Father."

Here is my life, a silk petal in Christ's bouquet, a daughter of the Most High.

Father, help our lives to be a sweet-smelling sacrifice to You.

RELATIONSHIPS

I have learned over the years that our relationship with our spouses is similar to that of our relationship to our Heavenly Father. If we do not communicate on a daily basis, we grow apart and get disconnected from the vine, so to speak. Marriage is a daily walk; sharing, caring, loving, forgiving and praying that keeps our hearts in tune with each other.

My husband and I just celebrated 22 years of marriage, some good and some not so good, and I can honestly say I love him more today than ever.

Falling in Love Over and Over

Our pastor once gave a message on marriage that has stuck with me through the hard times. He said a good marriage means falling in love over and over with the same person. I just love that saying.

Marriage is not about just feelings; it is a commitment. We do not always feel madly in love or happy with our spouses, but God honors our commitment and He restores the love we need in the rough times.

Without constant communication and prayer we grow apart instead of together as one. God's Word says,

> *...a man shall leave his father and mother and be joined to his wife, and they shall become one flesh.*
>
> (Genesis 2:24)

Our First Love

When we first fall in love with Jesus we cannot wait to talk to Him, to run to Him and tell Him everything, to spend time alone in His presence, to discover there is nothing He cannot take care of.

The Bible refers to God's Church as His Bride. The emotional "Wedding Song" speaks about the relationship between Christ and His Bride; *"My heart is stirred by a noble theme"* (Psalm 45:1, NIV). How happy our hearts are on that day, so full of love and joy, so hopeful, so enthralled with our future mate, optimistic, and ecstatic!

What is your heart yearning for today?

Oh God, help our hearts to remain steadfast in You. When everything else is constantly changing, You remain the same. Restore our first love with You and with our spouses. Bind and strengthen every marriage in my family with chords that cannot be broken.

My desire is like the song that says:

> *Just a closer walk with Thee, Lord,*
> *let it be. Dear Lord, let it be.*

(Anonymous)

MOTHER'S DAY

Today is Mother's Day. We have been honoring our sets of mothers several nights this week and it has been great. I have been the recipient of nearly a week-long celebration.

MY BABY'S COMING HOME

I am so excited on this particular Mother's Day, more so than I can remember for a long time, probably since the time my oldest daughter surprised me and had my first grandson dedicated on that special Sunday years ago.

My baby is coming home!

Truly, Sarah is not a baby anymore; she is a young woman almost 25 years of age, but still the baby to me. I am ecstatic!

ALWAYS THEIR MOTHER

I love being a mother, all its joys, heartaches, love and disappointments. It is a never-ending job, this title of being a "mother," because no matter how old your children are, you are ALWAYS their mother.

Our youth pastor, Greg, gave such a wonderful, touching message on the subject of mothers today. I felt so honored, so special, so privileged to carry this title. He gave affirmation to all the things that make mothers special.

I am so thankful to have been raised by a Christian mother and grandmothers. What a tremendous heritage for me! I have tried to pass that spiritual torch to my children, and I hope that I have modeled my life before them in a manner that leads them to Christ.

One of my favorite scriptures is,

> *Train up a child in the way he should go, and when he is old he will not depart from it.*
>
> (Proverbs 22:6)

BABY BUTTERFLIES

I do not know how to explain the relationship that begins the first time you feel those butterflies of your unborn child in your stomach. I know I felt like my feet were not touching the ground the rest of the day. When your child is born, you love them with everything within you, and even a little more.

I like what author Al Clarks says, "There is something inseparable between mother and child. Something forms as life begins and lives deep in the soil of the brain and heart, down where roots expand and cells divide, nurtured by blood."

It is just an amazing love, and it can only be so because of Christ's love for us. He imparts it to us and we pass it on. Just like the song:

> *Amazing love,*
> *how can it be,*
> *that you My King*
> *would die for me?*

(Words by Bill James Foote)

Such an awesome truth!

SACRIFICES AND SORROWS

I cannot imagine being the mother of Christ, the Savior of the world. What a special young woman she must have been for God to use her to carry His Son! I also cannot imagine the sacrifices and sorrows she bore when her child took the road to Golgotha, where He would lay down His life for you and for me.

As Jesus hung on the cross in his last hour on Earth, He reflected on His mother – what a wonderful example of the bond between mother and child.

Our children are a piece of our bodies, our souls, our spirits and our hearts, whether we bore them, adopted them, raised them – it does not matter how they come into our lives. Once they are there, they pull on the strings that forever bind us and they are a treasure of our life.

Whether they are starting their first day of pre-school or college it does not matter. Our worries, anxieties and prayers are always there.

OUR GOD-GIVEN RIGHT

I remember when my girls did not want me to walk them to or from elementary school anymore. We lived on the same street as their school and it was just a few blocks up. I would go out in the yard and hide behind the large bushes to watch them walk up the street. I would drive by the school during their recess time to catch a glimpse of them playing on the playground and then I would watch for them to come home.

Any of this sound familiar?

I bet it does.

We cannot help ourselves. It is our God-given right to love and care for our children that much.

How much more does our Heavenly Father care for us? Isaiah 66:13 says, *"As one whom his mother comforts, so I will comfort you..."*

Each time my oldest daughter, Paige, was carrying one of our grandchildren, a new bond formed between us. There is nothing like your child having a child. I know that it brought us closer in a new dimension. We became like best friends and she looked to me for guidance and advice like she did when she was a little girl.

I am so thankful today that as she and my son-in-law, Ryan, are raising their two boys, they are teaching them the joy of loving and serving the Lord and the privilege of prayer. I love that song that says:

May all those who come behind me find me faithful,
May the torch of my devotion light their way.

(Words by Jon Mohr)

TEACH YOUR CHILDREN WELL

Another favorite quote of mine is from Frederic Wertham who said, "A child's mind is like a bank. Whatever you put in it you get back in ten years, with interest." This is enough to cause us to ponder and consider carefully each day what we are teaching our children. May it be to love the Lord their God with all their hearts, souls and minds.

Clergyman Henry Ward Beecher said, "God pardons like a mother, who kisses the offense into everlasting forgiveness." May our children also learn that nothing they have done is too great an offense to be pardoned by our Father in Heaven, Who puts our transgressions as far from the East is from the West when we surrender our lives to Him.

KNITTING

I believe the inside of our heart is like a knitting process. The more people that we meet, the larger the knitting grows: more people to care for, to nurture, to love.

If you are anything like me, it is very hard to "drop a stitch" so to speak. Once I become involved in a person's life, I want to pray for them and I want them to know the same Jesus I know and love.

NEW STITCHES

When my husband and I got married, two more children were added to my life. They were treasures of my heart, just like my own two-year-old daughter, Sarah.

I love being a mother, I always have. It is a privilege and an awesome responsibility. It is not an easy job by far, and I know God gave me what I needed for each day: the strength to go on and comfort when things were not going so well.

The Bible says God will never leave us or forsake us and there were many days I desperately clung to that verse. Prayer to me was like an inner tube out in the ocean, a life saver when my own efforts seemed useless.

PRAYER CLOSET

I remember many days going into the bathroom to pray, to cry, to be alone. It was the only place I could get away from my three children, and even then usually one of the girls would knock on the door needing Mom for something or wanting to come in.

Now that they are older, they sometimes laugh remembering how Mom would use the bathroom to pray. I would kneel down on the floor, using the toilet to fold my hands on or lay my head on, and call out to God to help me when I felt I could not go on. I am so thankful for a merciful and loving Father who heard my cries, bottled up my tears and used them to replenish my spirit when it felt so dry.

God is so good. My heart can never thank Him enough for all He has done in my life. My soul doth magnify the Lord!

I like to think of the "stitches" as making a beautiful tapestry woven into my life. Who are the "stitches" in your life; the people in your circle that God has given you to care for? Think of them as a blanket you are weaving together. Cover them with a banner of love.

HEART'S TREASURES

Some of the greatest treasures of my heart are my grandchildren. I have two grandsons, Denver and Samuel, and I feel like my heart can barely contain all of the love I have for them. Before they were even born, I prayed for them faithfully, as I do now. I pray many blessings into their lives, but most of all I pray for them to grow to know Christ as Lord of their lives and to become great men of God.

THE TRUTHS I STAND ON

Grandchildren are such a blessing. It is our responsibility and awesome privilege as grandmothers to teach our grandchildren about Christ.

Only take heed to yourself, and diligently keep yourself, lest you forget the things your eyes have seen, and lest they depart from your heart all the days of your life. And teach them to your children and grandchildren.

(Deuteronomy 4:9)

Someday when I pass from this life to the next, I want my grandchildren to know what truths I stood on, what I believed in and who I served.

And I will pray the Father, and He will give you another helper, that He may abide with you forever – the Spirit of truth, whom the world cannot receive, because it neither sees Him nor knows Him; but you know Him, for he dwells with you and will be in you.

(John 14:16-17)

Blessed is the man who endures temptation; for when he has been approved, he will receive the crown of life which the Lord has promised to those who love Him.

(James 1:12)

And the Lord, He is the One who goes before you,
He will be with you. He will not leave you nor for-
sake you; do not fear nor be dismayed.
(Deuteronomy 31:8)

What legacy are we leaving our grandchildren?

May the footsteps that we leave cause them to believe and not to stumble.

NEVER ENOUGH

Is there some kind of timeline or standard of measurement that describes when you should release your children from your love and care?

When is it time to untie the strings of your heart like they were never attached and send your children soaring out into the world with never a care or feeling about their well-being?

For me, that time is never. As a mother, I pray for and over my children each and every day as well as for my son-in-law and grandchildren who have now been added into my life.

UNCONDITIONAL LOVE

God's love for us is unconditional; it is never ending just as our love for our children should be. That does not mean that they should not be taught to be independent and self-sufficient.

Likewise, Christians should not remain on "milk" but grow up in the strong meat of the Word of God.

God's love for us is always there. He promises to never leave or forsake us, and I believe that is how it should be for our children.

AN EXTENSION OF OUR LIVES

Just as Christ is the vine and we are the branches, our children are an extension of our lives. We hurt when they hurt. We rejoice when they reap blessings in their lives and our hearts and souls are connected just like we are to Christ. We are a family: people who love and care about each other just as those in the Body of Christ do.

Being in the family of God means you never have to be alone. You have brothers and sisters to lift your needs up before the throne of grace and to rejoice with you in times of blessing.

It is never enough to simply bring a child into this world, and it will never be time to stop loving them. God is love and therefore that is what our life should be about.

As newborn babes, desire the pure milk of the word, that you may grow thereby.

(1 Peter 2:2)

I will never leave you nor forsake you.

(Hebrews 13:5)

For as the body is one and has many members, but all the members of that one body, being many, are one body, so also is Christ.

(1 Corinthians 12:12)

I am the vine, you are the branches...

(John 15:5)

BROKEN HEART

Has your heart ever been broken? Mine has, about a "gazillion" times. You feel like you cannot breathe, it hurts so badly, and the pain is so intense you think it will never stop hurting.

As a little girl, I remember never wanting to disappoint my mother. If I did something to upset her and she decided to stop speaking to me, it would break my heart. I would go to my room and write her a note of apology and then be so happy when our normal relationship was restored.

I know that I have broken the heart of Christ so many times. Despite all the times I disappointed Him, let Him down, and failed Him, I also know how my heart has rejoiced when our relationship was restored and I knew I was once again walking in fellowship with Him.

UPS AND DOWNS

I am sure that just like me, you had your share of ups and downs in relationships where boys were concerned, and you often thought your heart would surely break in half, but you discovered that somehow life goes on.

I specifically remember one such occasion. I was having a birthday party at which my parents told me I could invite both boys and girls. At that time I had a crush on a certain boy. I used to imagine my first name with his last name, and would write it over and over. Have any of you ever done that?

Well, he never showed up for my party and my heart was broken. I got up the nerve to call his house only to find out his dad had made him stay home and to do yard work. It ruined my whole party! Even though I went on with a smile on my face, I was hurting.

There are other heart breaks along the way in life. We all experience them; death of loved ones, pets, rejection, whatever it may be.

Aching Hearts

I was fortunate enough to be blessed with some of the best fathers-in-law on earth. Ironically, two of them lived on the same street that I did at different times in my life. They were never too busy for me; they always had a smile and hearts of gold. Oh, how my heart was broken each time by their deaths.

The morning my husband found his dad at our family farm broke our hearts. He was taken from us in that quick moment of time without a good-bye and our hearts were aching. I still miss him terribly but the raw edges of pain and weeping are replaced with wonderful memories and love. I think losing my husband's dad reminded me to cherish those closest to me, to treasure them and not to take them for granted. Life is fragile and fleeting. Dad was very devoted to his family and he passed a torch on to each of us that are remaining and has brought us all closer together.

Wrapped in a Blanket of Love

I am so thankful that when the pain is so intense that we feel paralyzed, we can draw close to the Holy Spirit like a child does to its mother, so that we feel His presence ever-so-real, wrapping us in a blanket of warmth and love.

When trials and temptations attack our lives and wound our souls, we would do best to run to the Father.

God's Word tells us that in everything we are to give thanks, for this is His will (1 Thessalonians 5:18). Wow! In *everything*! That is a huge order to fill; to give thanks when our hearts are breaking, when our children are disobedient, when our spouse leaves us, and on and on it goes.

I love that song:

> *God answers prayer in the morning,*
> *God answers prayer through the day,*
> *God answers prayer in the evening,*
> *He hears you every time you pray.*

(Words by Ken Bible)

HOW COULD THIS HAPPEN TO ME?

Another time in my life that my heart was broken was the end of my first marriage. My heart kept asking, "How could this possibly be happening to me?" I was not only heartbroken; I was ashamed; humiliated to be labeled as a failure in the sanctity of marriage. I had been raised to believe God hates divorce, so you must work out your problems and never divorce.

I could not even say the word "divorce" for the longest time.

I had a small daughter to care for, so I began the process of job hunting. I remember filling out applications, and at interviews I could not bring myself to say the dreaded "D" word, so I would just say that I had a young daughter. The shame was overwhelming and my heart was broken.

I have never felt such intense pain and loss, and those of you who are reading this and have felt the "sting of divorce" know exactly what I am talking about. If you have children, you relive it with fresh wounds as they grow and the interaction is still there.

RUN TO THE FATHER'S ARMS

I clung desperately to my faith at that very dark time in my life and ran to the Father's arms for comfort and peace. It is heartbreaking to me to think of the scores of women out there that do not know the love of the Father. I honestly do not see how they can survive when the winds blow and the mountains crumble in our lives.

I love that song that says:

> *As the deer panteth for the water*
> *so my soul longeth after Thee.*
> *You alone are my heart's desire*
> *and I long to worship Thee.*
>   (Words by Martin Nystrom)

Oh, God I praise You for the strength and joy You have always been to me! Even when I rejected You, You were still there and You loved me in spite of myself. So many times You sheltered and protected me, even times that I am not aware of. How could my heart ever thank You enough for all You have done – even sending Your only Son to suffer and die the cruel death on the cross for one such as me.

My own children are the treasure of my heart; I cannot possibly begin to know the anguish of that day.

YOUR NAME IS LOVE

What a Savior I serve! Your name is love; You are love; that is why You require so much of us concerning love: to love one another, and the greatest commandment, to love the Lord our God with ALL of our hearts, souls, minds and strength and to love our neighbor as ourselves.

Loving someone as I do myself has always been hard for me to fully understand, to grasp. I think as a whole, people pretty much love themselves. We pamper our bodies, feed our minds with all kinds of things, and in general look out for number one — ourselves.

What does it really mean to love our neighbors as ourselves? Why would God ask this of us? *"Greater love has no man than to lay down his life for another"* – that is what Jesus did for us. He laid down His life for us even when we rejected Him, despised Him, did not know Him. He gave us everything so that we could have life.

Everything that we do for others pales in comparison to that great love.

Jesus paid it all; all to Him I owe. We owed a debt we could not pay; He paid a debt He did not owe.

Christ Jesus washed all our sins away.

Enter into His gates with thanksgiving, and into His court with praise. Be thankful to Him, and bless His name.

(Psalm 100:4)

125

LOCATION

ACROSS THE MILES

My son-in-law, Ryan, is a Captain in the U.S. Army, so his family is re-located every few years. They have lived in Ohio, Texas and Maryland, and their newest location is Savannah, Georgia.

The good news is that no matter where we are distance-wise in relationship to each other, as a family, our love reaches across the miles.

That is how it is with God. We can never be lost from Him. Wherever our travels in life may take us, He is always there.

What a comforting promise from God's Word: "I will never leave you nor forsake you" (Hebrews 13:5). Aren't you thankful for that?

This thought brings me to my daughter Sarah. She is currently living in Jacksonville, Florida pursuing a career in nursing. She has always been a step ahead of herself, pressing on to the next goal. Through the years I have watched her face adversity head on with so much strength that I wondered where it came from. She has so much spirit, drive and self-discipline and I am very thankful for the privilege of raising up such a beautiful daughter of His creation. We have evolved into a whole new relationship as she has grown and moved into her independence away from me but our hearts are forever knitted together with love. Every day I open my hands in prayer for her that God will lead, guide and direct her life. God's Word is true. Time and space mean nothing to Him. Just like that of a mother's love; it reaches across the miles. He has created everything for His glory, His purpose and His plan.

> *Be strong and of good courage, do not fear nor be afraid of them; for the Lord your God, He is the One who goes with you. He will not leave you nor forsake you*
>
> (Deuteronomy 31:6)

> *Lo, I am with you always, even to the end of the age.*
>
> (Matthew 28:20)

The next time your life becomes uprooted and you find yourself in a strange new environment; I hope you feel the presence of the One who is always with you.

People may not physically be able to see your heart but they know it by how you live your life. The things that we are the most passionate about, emotional about and set the highest on our priority list, reflect our character. People can "hear" our heart beating through our lives. I hope you desire to be a woman of faith and great purpose so that others can come to know the Father in all of His fullness.

I will give you a new heart and put a new spirit in you, I will take the heart of stone out of your flesh and give you a heart of flesh.

(Ezekiel 36: 26-27)

God Bless,

Debbie

NOTES FOR REFLECTION